The Development and Testing of Heckscher-Ohlin Trade Models

The Ohlin Lectures

The Development and Testing of Heckscher-Ohlin Trade Models:

A Review

Robert E. Baldwin

The MIT Press
Cambridge, Massachusetts
London, England

MIT Press books may be purchased at special quantity discounts for business or sales promotional use. For information, please e-mail special _sales@mitpress.mit.edu or write to Special Sales Department, The MIT Press, 55 Hayward Street, Cambridge, MA 02142.

This book was set in Palatino on 3B2 by Asco Typesetters, Hong Kong and was printed and bound in the United States of America.

Library of Congress Cataloging-in-Publication Data

Baldwin, Robert E.
The development and testing of Heckscher-Ohlin trade models : a review / Robert E. Baldwin.
  p. cm. — (Ohlin lectures)
Includes bibliographical references and index.
ISBN 978-0-262-02656-7 (hc : alk. paper) 1. International trade—Econometric models. I. Title.
HF1379.B355 2008
382.01'5195—dc22   2008016995

10 9 8 7 6 5 4 3 2 1

To Janice and our family

Contents

Preface

At the time I presented my Ohlin lectures in October 1993, the multi-factor, multi-good version of Heckscher-Ohlin trade theory (the Heckscher-Ohlin-Vanek model) was the dominant theoretical model of international trade. However, early empirical testing of the model based on multi-country, multi-factor data had yielded disappointing results. Thus, in addition to reviewing briefly both the theoretical development of this and related models and the results from these and other empirical tests, I discussed how modifying various assumptions of the model might yield a more complex but empirically satisfactory framework for understanding patterns of international trade. In particular, I emphasized an objective stressed by Ohlin, namely the need to formulate a dynamic model that integrated trade and development theory.

Empirical tests later in the 1990s strengthened the earlier conclusions about the shortcomings of the Heckscher-Ohlin-Vanek model. Trefler (1995) demonstrated that the volume of countries' trade predicted by this model was an order of magnitude greater than their measured trade and that the proportion of sign matches between predicted and measured trade in productive factors was no better than about 50 percent. While he showed that introducing Hicks-neutral technological differences among countries greatly improves the fit between predicted and measured trade, the basic Heckscher-Ohlin proposition concerning the importance of relative factor endowments still did not receive strong empirical support.

Fortunately, research in the late 1990s and early part of this decade by Davis and Weinstein (2001a) led to the formulation of a trade model that not only is strongly supported empirically but in which relative factor endowments play a major role. As explained in the text, the key was dropping the assumption of factor price equalization and permitting multiple cones of factor diversification in addition to introducing Hicks-neutral difference in technology among countries.

It struck me at the time that the contributions of these authors provided an appropriate occasion to review in greater detail the development and testing of Heckscher-Ohlin models since the publication of Ohlin's monograph in 1933. Consequently, with the encouragement of Elizabeth Murry, The MIT Press editor then handling the books based on authors' Ohlin lectures, I decided to revise and expand significantly the paper on which my lectures were based. The process has taken far longer than I expected, but it has been very satisfying personally to try put the various twists and turns that Heckscher-Ohlin trade theory and empirical testing has taken over the years into an understandable framework that shows how progress in this area of trade gradually took place. Unfortunately, now that I am retired, I have not had the opportunity to run the text by graduate students taking my course in international trade, who invariably are able to point out important omissions and errors in one's writings no matter how many times that the author has reviewed the text himself.

I am greatly indebted to two anonymous readers for The MIT Press who provided numerous valuable suggestions for improving the review. Mina Kim also provided valuable assistance in drawing the figures and in checking the text for grammar and typos.

In using a uniform notation in the various equations, I have mainly followed the style adopted by Rob Feenstra in his excellent graduate text in international trade.

December 2007
Madison, WI

1   Introduction

1.1   The Heckscher-Ohlin Proposition

It has been 75 years since the publication of Bertil Ohlin's (1933) pathbreaking treatise on interregional and international trade and nearly 90 years since the publication of the article by Ohlin's teacher, Eli Heckscher (1919), that significantly shaped Ohlin's thinking about trade theory.[1] No names are more closely associated with modern trade theory than those of Heckscher and Ohlin. As the basis for international trade, their model focuses on differences among countries in relative factor supplies and on differences among commodities in the intensities with which they use these factors. They show how differences in the relative supplies of factors of production influence the nature of intercountry differences in comparative costs under autarky conditions and explain how these differences affect not only the pattern of international trade but also factor prices and factor allocations in producing goods and services.[2] Furthermore Ohlin recognized that trade theory could be expressed in general equilibrium terms, where the prices and quantities of all goods and factors are determined simultaneously and the unsatisfactory real cost analysis of the classical model is avoided.

A century earlier David Ricardo (1817) had recognized that differences in comparative rather than absolute costs among countries are the basis of international trade and, therefore, that all countries can benefit from trade, even a country that is absolutely more productive in all goods. He did not investigate in any detail just why intercountry differences in comparative advantage arise, however. Intercountry differences in fixed-coefficient technology are simply assumed.

The basic Heckscher-Ohlin (HO) proposition about the nature of the commodity and the factor composition of interregional and international trade is as follows: "Roughly speaking, abundant industrial agents are relatively cheap, scanty agents relatively dear, in each region. Commodities requiring for their production much of the former and little of the latter are exported in exchange for goods that call for factors in the opposite proportions. Thus, indirectly, factors in abundant supply are exported and factors in scanty supply are imported." (Ohlin 1933, p. 92). It is the statement in the latter sentence that is referred to here as the basic HO proposition. General equilibrium theories in which relative factor endowments play an important role in determining the factor content of trade are termed to be HO trade models.

One of the reasons that Ohlin began this statement of the HO proposition with the phrase "roughly speaking" was his awareness that differences in relative factor prices under autarky conditions that would result just from differences in relative factor supplies could be offset by relative differences in consumer preferences for products between the two countries. For example, consumers in the country with the higher capital/labor endowment ratio could have such a strong preference for capital-intensive goods compared to the consumers of the labor-abundant country that, under autarky conditions, the prices of capital-intensive goods and thus the ratio of the return to capital to wages could be relatively higher in the capital-abundant country than the labor-abundant country. Consequently the opening of free trade between the two countries would result in the capital-abundant country importing capital-intensive goods and exporting labor-intensive goods. However, Ohlin (1933, pp. 16–17) believed that differences in relative factor endowments generally are more important than differences in relative preferences in shaping trade patterns.

Although Ohlin regarded differences in relative factor endowments as the main determinant of a country's pattern of trade, he did not regard them to be sufficiently important to justify focusing only on this relationship in theorizing about the nature of trade patterns or in empirically investigating them. He frequently emphasized the importance of scale economies in shaping the commodity composition of trade and sometimes put this relationship on an equal level of importance to that of relative factor endowments (Ohlin 1933, pp. 106–108; see earlier Ohlin 1924, p. 83, of the English translation of Ohlin's doctoral dissertation in Flam and Flanders 1991). He also emphasized the importance of qualitative differences in productive factors among countries, the use of entirely different technical processes of production by countries, intercountry variations in the stability of economic conditions, and different social conditions of production. Thus, apparently because he was concerned about abstracting too much from real world conditions, Ohlin did not formulate a simple factor proportions model with, for example, only two goods, two factors, and two countries. With such a model he could have much more readily investigated not only the assumptions necessary for the HO proposition to hold in a rigorous manner but also the possible effects of trade on factor prices.

In a mathematical appendix in which he explains how the factor proportions framework can be integrated into a general equilibrium pricing system, he does explicitly assume identical, constant returns-to-scale production functions in the two trading regions. However, in explaining the set of goods traded between the two countries, he assumes that each country specializes in a unique set of goods that are cheaper than in the other country at an exchange rate that balances the value of each country's exports and imports.[3] In modern terminology, he assumes that the two countries produce within different cones of factor diversification.[4] This enables Ohlin to avoid concluding, in contrast to Heckscher, that factor prices are equalized across countries with constant returns-to-scale production functions under free trade and no transportation costs. He apparently believed that factor price equalization was so unrealistic as a real world outcome that he did not want his theoretical framework to permit this possibility.

Ohlin's theory involves many productive factors and many goods, but it does not explain how the ordering of a country's ratios of its endowment of each factor to the world endowment of each factor is related to the ordering of the ratios of the country's net exports of each factor (embodied in goods) to the world endowment of each factor. Abundant factors are simply exported and scarce factors imported. It is not until Vanek's (1968) generalization to the many-factors, many-goods case that such an exact relationship is established.

In addition to adopting a very broad approach to analyzing the influences shaping trade patterns, Ohlin's analytical framework takes into account feedback effects of changes in trade on such determinants as the relative quantities and qualities of productive factors, the rate of technological change, the preferences of consumers, and the various economic and social institutions in each country. In other words, Ohlin explored not only the static general equilibrium effects of changes in the basic determinants of trade on the prices and outputs of both goods and factor services but also studied the dynamic implications of these effects on the quantitative and qualitative nature of the determinants as well. He did not attempt to undertake rigorous empirical tests of the HO proposition, however. Instead, Ohlin relied mainly on historical examples of the relationship among countries' trade patterns and their relative factor endowments to support this proposition.

The basic proposition set forth by Heckscher and Ohlin, namely that a country exports factors (embodied in goods) that are relatively abundant compared to the rest of the world and imports its relatively scarce factors, is still a key component of modern trade theory, but much has changed from Ohlin's analysis in *Interregional and International Trade* (1933) in terms of both theoretical formulation and empirical testing. Subsequent authors have not shown Ohlin's reluctance in making assumptions that result in factor price equalization and in constructing models from which strong, quantitative propositions about the predicted and actual factor content of trade can be rigorously derived (the Vanek theorem). In addition their models produce strong predictions about directional changes in factor prices as a consequence of changes in product prices (the Stolper-Samuelson theorem) and about directional changes in outputs in response to changes in relative factor supplies (the Rybczynski theorem). Indeed their theoretical contributions have been sufficiently significant that their names are often added to those of Heckscher and Ohlin in describing the model. For example, the familiar two-good, two-factor, two-country version is often referred to as the Heckscher-Ohlin-Samuelson (HOS) model in recognition of Samuelson's contributions in formulating the Stolper-Samuelson and factor price equalization theorems. The model that serves as the initial basis of most modern empirical trade tests is usually described as the Heckscher-Ohlin-Vanek (HOV) model in recognition of Vanek's contribution in formulating the theory in factor-content terms within a multi-good, multi-factor, multi-country framework. The key relationship of the HOV model is that the amount of a particular factor of production embodied (directly and indirectly) in a country's net trade of goods and services equals its endowment of this factor minus the world endowment of this factor multiplied by the country's share of the world's consumption of goods and services.

Analyses of situations in which factor price equalization does not occur under free trade have also been undertaken by trade economists (e.g., Jones 1956–57; Bhagwati 1972; Deardorff 1979; Brecher and Choudhri 1982b; Helpman 1984a). In his 1984 paper Helpman rigorously establishes a set of conditions concerning the factor content of *bilateral* trade patterns that *must* hold under free trade in a non–factor price equalization model without any restrictions on preferences. He does assume identical technologies between the countries, however. Interestingly this is the model that Ohlin set forth in his mathematical appendix. Although

Helpman points out that his predictions should prove useful in empirical tests of factor proportions trade theory, it has only been within recent years that they have been used for this purpose. (His model is described in detail in chapter 2, and the empirical evaluation of the model by Choi and Krishna 2004 is discussed in chapter 4.)

1.2 General Purpose and Some Conclusions

In this book I review both the theoretical development of the basic insights of Heckscher and Ohlin into the modern factor-content trade model and the results of empirical tests of HO models.[5] I devote particular attention to examining the extent to which the factor-content version of the HO proposition is supported in these empirical tests. I also examine the results from investigating other predictions of HO models, in particular, the search for Stolper-Samuelson, Rybczynski, and factor price equalization effects. My general purpose is to evaluate how well the formulation and testing of HO models have succeeded in improving our understanding of the forces shaping international trade and its economic impact.

My basic conclusion on this matter is that we have made considerable theoretical and empirical strides over the last fifty or so years in improving our understanding of the economic forces affecting the factor trade embodied in traded commodities. However, it does appear that most empirical trade economists (myself included) became overfascinated with the elegant but highly unrealistic factor price equalization models developed from the insights of Heckscher and Ohlin to the detriment of empirically investigating other theoretical models without this relationship. Since bilateral tests involving the United States and the rest of the world produced mixed results with regard to the HO proposition, leading empirical trade economists began to devote much of their efforts to assembling detailed multi-country data sets on trade and factor endowments in order to tie the tests of the HO proposition to the basic HOV model. The tests revealed little support for the HO proposition that countries export their relatively abundant factors (embodied in goods) and import their relatively scarce productive factors. Specifically, they showed that the signs predicted by the HOV model for the net exports of productive factors matched the signs of measured net exports of these factors in only about 50 percent of the cases, or by the proportion one would expect simply by chance. More detailed analysis also revealed that the measured net trade embodied in productive factors is an order of magnitude smaller than predicted by the basic HOV equation: there is a huge gap between the amount of factor trade predicted by the equation and the actual factor trade measured by researchers. This gap has been described by Trefler (1995) as "the case of the missing trade."

These economists then sought to determine if they could account for the very poor performance of the HOV model by introducing a few econometrically simple modifications of its assumptions that would lead both to a much better quantitative fit between the actual and predicted factor content of trade and to an increase in the proportion of sign matches between the predicted and actual factor content of trade. Introducing "best-fit" Hicks-neutral differences in factor efficiency among countries is an appealing modification, since factor price equalization in efficiency units still exists with this modification. As I show in detail in chapter 4, introducing this modification significantly reduces the amount of missing trade. However, it does not appreciably improve the results of the basic test of the HO proposition with regards to the proportion of sign matches between the predicted and actual factor content of trade.

It is only when the assumptions of the HOV model are further modified to yield nonuniform differences among factor input requirements within and among countries (see the discussion in chapter 4 of Davis and Weinstein 2001a) that there is also strong support for the HO proposition.[6] The modification by these authors involves introducing both Hicks-neutral estimates of intercountry efficiency differences based on their data set and observed differences in capital/labor endowment ratios among countries as indicators of the extent to which industry factor inputs differ across countries.[7] This matching of the predicted and actual factor content of trade in an accounting sense is an ingenious accomplishment, but the resulting model is very different from the HOV model with factor price equalization from which they started. Although the successive modifications help account for why the HOV model fails, the basic reasons why factor efficiency differences occur or why multiple cones of factor diversification arise are not explained. Although we end up concluding that relative factor endowments matter in accounting for the embodied factor content of trade, there remains a black box of other important forces influencing this trade whose components and determinants are not well understood. Further research efforts directed at formulating and testing theories dealing with these determinants are very much needed.

In hindsight, in investigating the empirical relationship between relative factor endowments and the factor content of international trade, it may have been more productive to place greater emphasis on the non–factor price equalization model investigated by Brecher and Choudhri (1982b), more fully developed by Helpman (1984a), and finally tested by Choi and Krishna (2004). This might have avoided what seems to have been excessive attention on trying to account for the "missing trade" that is a key result of strong tests of the unmodified HOV model. Efforts might have been devoted earlier to such highly relevant topics of recent empirical research as testing for the existence and number of cones of diversification (e.g., Schott 2003a, b), the exchange of factor services involved in intra-industry trade (e.g., Davis and Weinstein 2001b), and the importance of economies of scale (e.g., Antweiler and Trefler 2002; Davis and Weinstein 2003).

The heavy focus on the HOV model may also help explain why trade economists have not devoted as much attention as Ohlin to the dynamic feedback effects of trade on such basic determinants as the quantity and quality of productive factors and the state of technology. Perhaps the prospects that an analysis of these effects would not yield such sweeping and sharp economic conclusions as has emerged from the static HOV framework have served to discourage research along these lines. Probably a more important explanatory factor, however, is the long tradition of classical and neoclassical economists of analyzing international trade mainly in comparative static terms.

While there have been important exceptions to the usual comparative statics approach to trade theory (e.g., see Grossman and Helpman 1991), trade economists need to devote more attention to the effects of trade on technological conditions, on the domestic supplies and international movements of capital and labor as well as on such factors as consumer tastes, the competitive nature of markets, and the nature of economic institutions. By not analyzing the dynamic effects of trade with the same depth as they analyze their static determinants, trade economists tend to underemphasize the manner in which trade influences the nature of an economy's development over time and the policy issues that affect this matter. In my view, Ohlin rightly took a much broader view of the conditions determining the commodity patterns of trade compared to most modern analysts of the subject and correctly stressed more strongly how the feedback effects of trade, in turn, affect the nature of these conditions. Of course, while it is easy to discuss such matters qualitatively, the real need is for rigorous analytical results that lead to sensible empirical results.[8]

The study is organized in the following manner. Chapter 2 briefly surveys the development of HO trade theory. No attempt is made to undertake a full and detailed history of economic thinking on HO models. The chapter simply presents the perspective of one academic who has observed much of the development of these models as it occurred. As will be explained, key scholars involved in the formulation and extension of the primary proposition of Heckscher and Ohlin into a two-good, two-factor, two-country general equilibrium model were Stolper and Samuelson (1941), Samuelson (1948, 1949, 1953–54), and Jones (1965a). Travis (1964), Melvin (1968), and especially Vanek (1968) then played key roles in generalizing this model into the modern multi-good, multi-factor, multi-country factor-content HOV model. As the chapter emphasizes, these extensions of the basic intuitions of Heckscher and Ohlin into an elegant, yet simple general equilibrium model with strong relationships between relative factor supplies of countries, relative prices and outputs of the goods they produce, and the relative returns earned by the productive factors represent a major accomplishment in trade theory. They quickly replaced the real cost approach that had long dominated the modeling of the causes and consequences of international trade. The non–factor price equalization model of Helpman (1984a), which builds on earlier work by Brecher and Choudri (1982b), is also discussed in the chapter.

Chapters 3 and 4 review and critique empirical tests of the basic HO proposition, which states that a country exports factors (embodied in goods) that are relatively abundant compared to the rest of the world and imports its relatively scarce factors. Chapter 3 covers the early period of testing beginning with Leontief's famous 1953 paper to about the mid-1980s during which trade economists mainly measured the factor content of a single country's trade with the rest of the world for only two or three productive factors. Particular attention is devoted to the so-called Leontief paradox. Chapter 4 then examines test results of the HO proposition in a multi-factor, multi-country framework that began with Maskus (1985) and Bowen, Leamer, and Sveikauskas (1987) and have continued to be carried out by Trefler (1993, 1995), Davis and Weinstein (2001a), and others. This chapter also focuses on empirical tests of the basic HOV relationship that the amount of a particular factor of production embodied (directly and indirectly) in a country's net trade of goods and services equals its endowment of this factor minus its share of world consumption times the world endowment of this factor. Among other topics covered are country-pair tests of the HO proposition and empirical investigations into the importance of intra-industry trade and increasing returns. The test of Helpman's (1984a) non–factor price equalization model undertaken by Choi and Krishna (2004) is also reviewed in this chapter.

Chapter 5 reviews selected empirical investigations of the other basic propositions of the HO model, namely, the Stolper-Samuelson, Rybczynski, and factor price equalization theorems. Chapter 6 then concludes with a brief summary of what we have learned from the various empirical tests and a discussion of lines of research topics that seem to warrant greater attention in the future.

2 The Development of Heckscher-Ohlin Trade Models

2.1 Trade Theory in the 1930s

Although Heckscher published his seminal article, "The Effect of Foreign Trade on the Distribution of Income," in 1919 and the essential theoretical parts of Ohlin's 1933 book, *Interregional and International Trade*, are contained in his 1924 PhD thesis, *The Theory of Trade*, the fact that these early contributions were published in Swedish seems to account for their failure to have much influence on other European or North American trade economists of this period. It was not until the latter 1930s that Ohlin's ideas about the importance of relative factor proportions in influencing the composition of a country's trade began to appear in textbooks on international trade (e.g., Ellsworth 1938). Moreover the rigorous formulation of the two-good, two-factor, two-country model in which both production and distribution conditions could be easily analyzed did not begin to take shape until the 1941 article by Stolper and Samuelson, which set forth their famous theorem.

The major development in trade theory in the 1930s was the displacement of the classical "real cost" doctrine that dominated international economics through the 1920s by

the "opportunity cost" approach first extended to trade
theory by Haberler (1936).[1] This change represented a shift
in emphasis from the welfare side of trade to the positive
side of modeling how prices and quantities are determined
in a trading framework with more than one factor and with
variable factor proportions in production.[2] A two-good
geometrical representation of a country's opportunity cost
curve (now more commonly called, the production possibilities curve or frontier) indicates the minimal reduction in the
quantity of one good needed to secure an extra unit of the
other good by redistributing the given supply of productive
factors between the goods. Adding a set of community indifference curves between the two goods (see Lerner, 1932,
1934 and Leontief, 1933) soon became the standard way of
showing the derivation of a country's reciprocal demand or
offer curve. By matching the home country's offers of one
good for the other good at different relative prices against a
foreign country's offers of the second good for the first good
at different relative prices, the market-clearing equilibrium
relative price of the goods and the volume of trade between
the two countries can be determined. Placing this equilibrium trading line into a figure depicting the home country's
production possibilities curve such that the trading line
is tangent to both the production possibilities curve and an
indifference curve then indicates the home country's equilibrium production and consumption points for the two
goods.[3]

2.2 The Heckscher-Ohlin-Samuelson (HOS) Model

Although not generally recognized initially, Samuelson
(1938) pointed out that Haberler's opportunity cost approach does not conflict with Ohlin's general equilibrium

approach but is rather a component part of such a model. This recognition facilitated the remarkably noncontroversial development by trade economists of the two-good, two-factor, two-country HOS model. The model is described here by reviewing its four basic theorems: the Stolper-Samuelson, Rybczynski, factor price equalization, and HO theorems.

2.2.1 The Stolper-Samuelson Theorem

The key step in the development of a formal general equilibrium model was taken by Stolper and Samuelson (1941) who utilized a two-good, two-factor framework to analyze the effects of an increase in the price of one of the goods relative to the other on the returns to the two productive factors employed within a country. Assuming fixed factor supplies that are perfectly mobile within the country but completely immobile internationally, perfect competition in domestic factor and product markets, and constant returns-to-scale technology for producing the two goods, these authors established that an increase in the relative price of one of the goods increases the real reward of the factor used relatively intensively in the production of that good and decreases the real reward of the other factor.[4]

In the diagrammatic analysis included in their article, Stolper and Samuelson ingeniously modified the Bowley-Edgeworth box diagram that depicts the optimal set of distributions of given total quantities of two goods between two consumers (in the sense of maximizing the welfare level of each consumer, given a particular and feasible welfare level for the other consumer) who have different, convex (to the origin of each consumer's indifference map), sets of indifference curves that do not intersect. The authors used

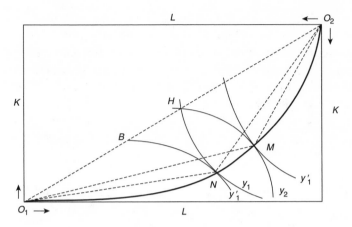

Figure 2.1 Stolper-Samuelson box diagram

the diagram to depict the sets of equal-output curves (isoquants) for two goods produced in a country under constant returns-to-scale conditions with different combinations of given and fully employed quantities of two factors of production.

The Stolper-Samuelson diagrammatic demonstration of the theorem are shown in figures 2.1 and 2.2. Since these two basic diagrams are used to illustrate all four theorems of the HOS model, it may be helpful to review briefly the basic relationships that exist in the diagrams. The point O_2 (the upper right-hand corner) in the factor endowments box in figure 2.1 indicates the total quantities of capital K and labor L available in the economy (as measured from point O_1) that can be distributed between the production of goods 1 and 2. The capital/labor endowment ratio for the country, K/L, equals the slope of the dashed diagonal line O_1BHO_2. The isoquant curves y_1 and y_1', which are convex to the

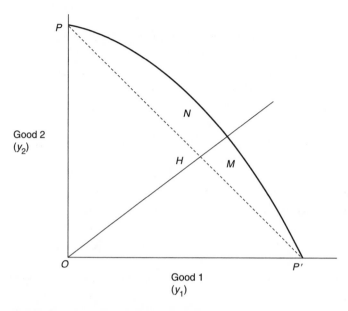

Figure 2.2 Production-possibilities curve

origin O_1, each indicate combinations of capital and labor (measured in a northeast direction) that yield equal outputs of good 1, with the output of good 1 being greater on the y_1' isoquant than on the y_1 isoquant along any constant K/L line. Similarly the isoquant curves y_2 and y_2', which are convex to their origin O_2, each show combinations of capital and labor (measured in a southwest direction) that yield equal outputs of good 2. Again, measured from O_2 as the origin, the output of good 2 on the y_2' isoquant is greater than on the y_2 isoquant along any constant K/L line. The locus of tangencies of such isoquants, the curve O_1NMO_2 or the Pareto efficiency locus, shows the maximum output level possible for each good, given a particular and feasible output level for the other good. The outputs of the two goods along this curve indicate the country's optimum production levels and are depicted in figure 2.2 as the production possibilities curve $PNMP'$.

At point O_1 in figure 2.1, all of the country's capital and labor are employed in producing good 2, and at point O_2, all the capital and labor are devoted to the production of good 1. Both goods are produced at points N and M on the Pareto efficiency locus with more of good 2 and less of good 1 being produced at N than at M. The slope of the line O_1N in figure 2.1 equals the capital/labor ratio used in producing good 1 at N, while the slope of O_2N (measured from O_2) equals the capital/labor ratio used in producing good 2 at N. Because the Pareto efficiency locus O_1NMO_2 lies below the diagonal O_1BHO_2, good 1 uses capital less intensively than good 2 at all points on the optimal production curve. If, however, the Pareto efficiency locus lies above the diagonal, good 1 is the capital-intensive good. A Pareto efficiency line that lies along the diagonal indicates that the capital/labor ratio used in producing the two goods is the same.

Due to the assumption of linear, homogeneous production functions, the slopes of the isoquants for, say, good 1 $\Delta K_1/\Delta L_1$ or the technical rate of substitution of capital for labor holding the output of good 1 constant, are the same along a constant capital/labor proportion line (the line O_1N in figure 2.1). The absolute marginal productivities of each factor are also fixed along any given capital/labor ratio line with equal distances along such a line representing equal amounts of output of the good. Furthermore increasing the capital/labor ratio used in producing a good lowers the marginal productivity of capital in the good's production and raises the marginal productivity of labor.

Because the output of good 1 (good 2) remains unchanged in a movement along any of good 1's (good 2's) isoquants, (minus) the slopes of the isoquants equal the ratio of the marginal productivities of the two factors. Thus

$$-\left(\frac{\Delta K_1}{\Delta L_1}\right) = \frac{MP_{L1}}{MP_{K1}}, \tag{2.1a}$$

$$-\left(\frac{\Delta K_2}{\Delta L_2}\right) = \frac{MP_{L2}}{MP_{K2}} \tag{2.1b}$$

where MP_{L1} and MP_{L2} are the marginal productivities of labor for goods 1 and 2, respectively, and MP_{K1} and MP_{K2} are the marginal productivities of capital for goods 1 and 2, respectively.

Also, since the price of each factor equals the value of its marginal product under perfectly competitive market conditions, the following condition holds:

$$w = p_2 MP_{L2} = p_1 MP_{L1},$$

$$r = p_2 MP_{K2} = p_1 MP_{K1}, \tag{2.2}$$

where w and r are the wages of labor and the return to capital, respectively, and p_1 and p_2 are the prices of goods 1 and 2, respectively.

If the isoquant systems for goods 1 and 2 are not equal (in the sense of the slopes of the two isoquant systems not being identical along any constant capital/labor proportion line), a representation in goods 1 and 2 output space of the quantities produced (denoted as y_1 and y_2 in figure 2.2) along the Pareto efficiency locus O_1NMO_2 in figure 2.1 yields a production possibility frontier that is concave to the origin (e.g., the curve $PNMP'$ in figure 2.2).[5] If, however, the isoquant systems for the two goods are identical, their locus of tangencies lie along the diagonal, O_1BHO_2, in figure 2.1, and this is represented in figure 2.2 by the line PHP'.

This latter line indicates a constant marginal opportunity cost of producing each good in the sense that a small increase in the output of one good involves a given constant decrease in the output of the other good. In contrast, optimal expansion curves that are uniformly below or above the diagonal in figure 2.1 (depending on which good has the higher capital/labor ratio at all points along the optimum expansion path) yield a concave (to their origin) production possibility frontier (such as $PNMP'$ in figure 2.2) with an increasing marginal opportunity cost of production for each good.[6] In other words, as the output of one good is increased, an increasing amount of the other good must be forgone to obtain an additional unit of the first good. When both goods are produced under perfectly competitive market conditions, the marginal cost of producing one good in terms of the other—namely (minus) the slope of the production possibility frontier—equals the ratio of the prices of the two goods, or

$$-\left(\frac{\Delta y_2}{\Delta y_1}\right) = \frac{p_1}{p_2}. \tag{2.3}$$

The Stolper-Samuelson theorem follows in a straightforward manner from these various relationships. The key is that the optimal capital/labor ratios used in producing given quantities of each good change in the same direction as the output of one good increases and the other decreases. Assume, for example, that there is a rise in the price of good 1 (with the price of good 2 being held constant) that leads to a shift of capital and labor from the production of good 2 to the production of good 1. Such a reallocation of a country's fixed supply of capital and labor is illustrated in figure 2.1 by the movement from N to M on the Pareto efficiency locus O_1NMO_2 and in figure 2.2 from N to M on the production possibilities frontier $PNMP'$. Since the line O_1M in figure 2.1 is steeper than the line O_1N and since the line O_2M (as measured from O_2 as the origin) is steeper than the line O_2N (and also steeper than the diagonal O_1BHO_2, which indicates the capital/labor ratio for the economy as a whole), the capital/labor ratios utilized in the production of both goods are greater at M than at N. Consequently, because the marginal productivity of labor is higher and the marginal productivity of capital lower at point M than N in terms of both goods, the real wages of labor rise unambiguously and the real return to capital falls.

The economic intuition for the process that takes place is as follows: Because good 1 utilizes a lower capital/labor ratio than good 2, the proportion of capital and labor optimally needed to expand the production of good 1 at given relative factor prices is less than the proportion released from sector 2 as its production decreases. The excess supply of capital and excess demand for labor cause the real return to capital to decrease and real wages to increase. Capital is substituted for labor in producing both goods in response to this change in relative factor prices, and the capital/labor ratio increases in both sectors. As Jones (1965a) points out, there is a "magnification effect" whereby (in the example considered above) wages rise proportionately more than the price of good 1 and, of course, relative to the unchanged price of good 2, while the returns to capital fall relative to the prices of both goods 1 and 2.

As Stolper and Samuelson explain, the reason algebraically for this counterintuitive relationship (how can the capital/labor ratio used in producing both goods rise, while the capital/labor ratio for the country as a whole remain unchanged?) is that the capital/labor ratio for the country as a whole, namely K/L, is a weighted average of the capital/

labor ratios used in producing each good, namely K_1/L_1 and K_2/L_2, where the weights are the proportions of the country's total labor used in producing each good, namely L_1/L and L_2/L. In equation terms,

$$\frac{K}{L} = \frac{L_1}{L} \cdot \frac{K_1}{L_1} + \frac{L_2}{L} \cdot \frac{K_2}{L_2}. \tag{2.4}$$

Simplifying the notation in this equation by letting L_1/L and L_2/L be represented by l_1 and l_2, respectively (where $l_1 + l_2 = 1$), K_1/L_1 and K_2/L_2 be represented by k_1 and k_2, respectively, and K/L by k, the equation can be written as

$$k = l_1 k_1 + l_2 k_2. \tag{2.5}$$

In the case discussed above where the output of good 1 increases and good 2 decreases, the first term on the right-hand side of the equation increases (as both l_1 and k_1 increase), whereas the second term decreases as k_2 rises and l_2 falls with k remaining unchanged.

In illustrating the policy relevance of their theorem, the authors assume that the relatively capital-intensive good 2 is exported and the relatively labor-intensive good 1 imported under free trade conditions. They then assume that the domestic price of the import good 1 increases relative to the price of the export good in response to an import restriction (such as an import duty). The output of good 1 therefore increases while the output of good 2 decreases. Thus, as described in the preceding paragraphs, real wages rise and the real return to capital falls as a result of this protectionist action.

The significance of this result for trade policy was not immediately fully appreciated even by the authors. They merely conclude: "We have shown that there is a grain of truth in the pauper labor type of protection." In rejecting publication of the paper in the *American Economic Review*, the editors informed the authors: "We both agree that the article is a brilliant theoretical performance...."[7] However, later in the letter, they stated: "On the other hand, we agree that it is a very narrow study in formal theory, which adds practically nothing to the literature of the subject with which it is nominally concerned." Fortunately, Ursula Hicks at the *Review of Economic Studies* thought otherwise and, in accepting the paper for publication, congratulated Stolper "... on having found a new point in the theory of international trade."

The authors' elaboration of their theorem within the context of the issue of the effect of import protection on real wages has led to the widespread association of the Stolper-Samuelson theorem with discussions of trade polices. Indeed, as Deardorff (1994) points out in his overview of the Stolper-Samuelson theorem, two versions of the theorem are stated in terms of trade policy. One, first described by Bhagwati (1959) as the "general" version states: "An increase in protection raises the real wage of the scarce factor of production and lowers the real wage of the abundant factor of production." (Deardorff 1994, p. 12). A second, referred to by Bhagwati (1957) as the "restrictive" version can be stated as: "Free trade lowers the real wage of the scarce factor and raises that of the abundant factor compared to autarky." (Deardorff 1994, p. 12). Deardorff termed the version stated at the outset of this subsection that "an increase in the relative price of one of the goods increases the real reward of the factor used relatively intensively in the production of that good and decreases the real reward of the other factor," as the "essential" version and noted that it is the one most frequently cited in analyses of the HOS model. Stolper and Samuelson clearly recognized the generality of the theorem by stating: "It is irrelevant for our argument just why the exchange ratio of the two commodities is different after international trade is established; it is sufficient that it does change (Stolper and Samuelson 1941, p. 34).[8]

As Stolper and Samuelson recognized, their theorem does not generalize well when the number of productive factors is increased beyond two. A number of trade theorists have investigated the conditions and senses in which the theorem can be generalized (see Chipman 1969; Kemp and Wegge 1969; Ethier 1974, 1982, 1983; Jones and Scheinkman 1977; Jones 1985).[9] Two generalizations are most widely cited in modern discussions of the theorem. The first is the "friends" and "enemies" version set forth first by Ethier (1974) and generalized (and named) by Jones and Scheinkman (1977). To quote Ethier (1983, p. 543): "An increase in the price of an initially produced good using a nonspecific assortment of at least two factors necessarily causes some factor reward to rise in even greater proportion and some factor reward to fall." It should be noted that one cannot specify which factor of production experiences an increase in its real reward or which undergo a decline in its real return. A "correlation" version, also first pointed out by Ethier (1982), can be expressed as follows (see Deardorff 1994, p. 18): "For any vector of goods price changes, the accompanying vector of factor price changes will be positively correlated with the factor-intensity-weighted averages of the goods price changes." This version provides the basis for a widely used method of empirically testing the theorem in a many-goods, many-factors framework.

2.2.2 *The Rybczynski Theorem*

Whereas the Stolper-Samuelson theorem focuses on the factor price effects within a country of a change in the relative price of one of the goods produced under fixed factor supply conditions, the Rybczynski (1955) theorem examines the relative output effects within a country of a change in the supply of one of its productive factors under fixed relative product-price conditions.[10] In the two-good, two-factor HOS model, the theorem states that an increase in the supply of one factor, with product prices held constant, increases the output of the product using this factor intensively and decreases the output of the other product. As with the Stolper-Samuelson theorem, the Rybczynski theorem assumes unchanged constant returns-to-scale technology, perfect competition, and incomplete specialization.[11]

The theorem can easily be explained using the Stolper-Samuelson box diagram and the depiction of the production possibilities frontier described in illustrating the Stolper-Samuelson theorem. In figure 2.3 the point O_2 represents the same total quantities of labor and capital as available to the country initially. The curve O_1NO_2 is the same Pareto

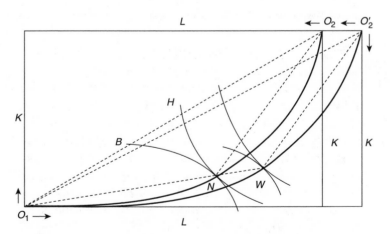

Figure 2.3 Rybczynski effects in Stolper-Samuelson diagram

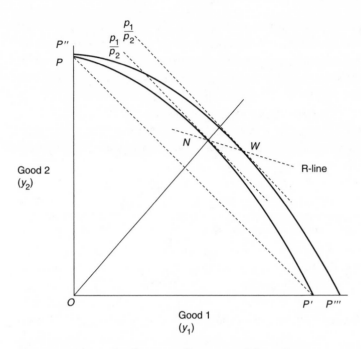

Figure 2.4 Rybczynski effects in production-possibilities diagram

efficiency locus depicted in figure 2.1 as O_1NMO_2. Similarly
the capital/labor ratio used in producing good 1 at point
N in figure 2.3 is indicated by the slope of the line O_1N
and the capital/labor ratio utilized in producing good 2 is
shown by the slope of the line O_2N (measured from the origin O_2). The outputs of goods 1 and 2 at N in figure 2.1 are
also represented in figure 2.4 as the point N on the production possibilities frontier PNP' (shown in figure 2.2 as
$PNMP'$). Assume that point N in figure 2.4 is the initial production equilibrium point for the country. Then the slope
of the production possibilities frontier $\Delta y_2/\Delta y_1$ at N is equal
to (minus) the equilibrium price ratio of good 1 to good 2,

$-(p_1/p_2)$. The (minus) slope of the p_1/p_2 line in figure 2.4 that is tangent to the production possibilities frontier at N indicates this equilibrium price of good 1 in terms of good 2.

Now assume that there is an increase in the country's supply of labor equal to the quantity represented by O_2O_2' in figure 2.3, without any change in its supply of capital. The total labor and capital supplies of the country in period 2 are indicated by the point O_2' in the diagram, with the country's set of isoquants for good 2 now being measured in a southwest direction from the new origin at O_2'. Consequently all isoquants for good 2 in the original box diagram are moved to the right by the distance O_2O_2', while those for good 1 are unchanged and still measured in a northeast direction with O_1 as the origin. This means that the slopes of good 2 isoquants along the line $O_2'W$, which is drawn parallel to the line O_2N, are the same as the slopes of good 2 isoquants in the initial box along the line O_2N in figure 2.3. Because the origin of the good 1 isoquant system is still O_1, the slopes of this good's isoquants along the extension of the line O_1N to O_1NW remain unchanged. Thus at the point W the slope of the good 1 isoquant passing through this point is the same as the slope of the good 2 isoquant passing through the point N. Therefore the Pareto efficiency locus with the increased supply of labor passes through W and the marginal productivities of labor and capital for both goods and the marginal cost of good 1 in terms of good 2 are the same as at point N. Since N is assumed to be the equilibrium allocation of capital and labor at the initial price ratio for the two goods, W indicates the equilibrium capital and labor allocation with the same product-price ratio with a larger supply of labor.

The Rybczynski relationship is evident in figure 2.3 because the output of a good at a point along a constant

capital/labor proportion line is proportional to the length of
the line from its origin. Since the constant capital/labor proportion line O_1NW is longer from O_1 to W than from O_1 to
N, the output of good 1 is obviously greater at W than at N.
Moreover, because of its positive slope, the line O_1NW
intersects the line $O_2'W$ at a point where the length of this
latter line from its origin O_2' is less than the length of the
parallel line O_2N from its origin O_2. Thus the increased labor supply, given a fixed amount of capital and unchanged
prices of goods 1 and 2, increases the output of the good
intensively using labor, namely good 1, and decreases the
output of good 2. As pointed out by Jones (1965a), there is
also a "magnification effect" with the Rybczynski theorem
in the sense that the output of the good intensively using
the factor whose supply has increased rises proportionately
more than the supplies of both productive factors, while the
output of the other good decreases proportionately more
than the supplies of both factors.[12]

Equation 2.4 above can also be used to illustrate the Rybczynski theorem. As noted in discussing this equation, it can
be simplified by letting L_1/L and L_2/L be represented by l_1
and l_2, respectively (where $l_1 + l_2 = 1$), K_1/L_1 and K_2/L_2 by
k_1 and k_2, respectively, and K/L by k. Thus, as previously
shown, it can be written as follows:

$$k = l_1k_1 + l_2k_2, \tag{2.5}$$

or, because $l_2 = 1 - l_1$, as

$$k = l_1(k_1 - k_2) + k_2. \tag{2.6}$$

In the Rybczynski example discussed above, where the
country's supply of labor is increased but its supply of capital and prices of goods 1 and 2 (and thus k_1 and k_2) are held
constant, the decrease in the country's capital/labor endow-

ment ratio k, must lead to an increase in l_1, since $(k_1 - k_2)$ is assumed to be negative. Devoting a larger proportion of an increased labor supply to the production of good 1 (as well as shifting part of the given capital supply out of the production of good 2 and into the production of good 1 in order to hold k_1 constant) obviously increases the output of good 1 and decreases the output of good 2.

These output changes are depicted in terms of production-possibilities frontiers in figure 2.4, where the point N on the production-possibilities frontier PNP' indicates the initial equilibrium production point for goods 1 and 2 at the given product price ratio p_1/p_2. The curve $P''WP'''$ is the production possibilities frontier after the increase in the supply of capital, and W is the new equilibrium production point where the slope of the production frontier $P''WP'''$ at W is the same as at N on the initial production-possibilities curve. Thus the price line p_1/p_2 that is tangent to the new production possibilities curve at W is parallel to the price line tangent to the initial production-possibilities curve at N. As shown in figure 2.4, the equilibrium output of good 1 increases, while the output of good 2 decreases. The dashed line passing through points M and W is the so-called Rybczynski line (labeled as the R-line in figure 2.4) and is the locus of tangencies between production possibilities frontiers formed by changing the supply of labor in figure 2.3 while holding the supply of capital and the product price ratio p_1/p_2 constant.[13] The line is straight, since output per unit of labor is a linear function of the capital/labor ratio in the HOS model.

Equations (2.5) and (2.6) also reveal a more general version of the Rybczynski theorem. In the two-good, two-factor HOS model, an increase in the supply of one factor relative to the other, with product prices held constant, increases the output of the product using this factor intensively relative to the output of the other product. A country's capital/labor factor endowment ratio k can decline, for example, even if the supplies of capital as well as labor increase absolutely, provided the absolute supply of capital increases proportionately less than the labor supply. With k_1 and k_2 held constant (where $k_2 > k_1$) in equation (2.6), the proportion of the labor supply devoted to the production of good 1, l_1, must increase when k decreases. This increase in l_1 increases the output of good 1. However, although the proportion of the labor supply devoted to the production of good 2, l_2, decreases (since $l_2 = 1 - l_1$), the output of good 2 can rise in absolute terms because of the increased labor supply (but not proportionately as much as good 1). A variation of this relationship is used in the next section in explaining the HO theorem.

As is the situation with the Stolper-Samuelson theorem, the Rybczynski theorem does not generalize well when the number of goods and factors exceed two. The following statement by Ethier (1983, p. 544) summarizes the limited relationship that holds in these circumstances: "At constant factor prices, an increase in the endowment of a non-specific factor used in at least two sectors, which leaves that factor fully employed, produces a more than proportional rise in the output of some good and a fall in the output of some other good." Ethier (1984, p. 168) also points out that a correlation version of the Rybczynski theorem holds analogous to the correlation version of the Stolper-Samuelson theorem, namely that "endowment changes tend on average to increase the most those goods making relatively intensive use of those factors which have increased the most in supply." However, unlike in the Stolper-Samuelson case, factor price equalization is required, which is of practical significance only if the number of goods is equal to or greater than the number of factors.

A reciprocity relationship between the Stolper-Samuelson and Rybczynski propositions first pointed out by Samuelson (1953–1954) and later elaborated by Jones (1965a,b) is that a rise in the price of a commodity produces the same effect on a factor reward as a rise in the endowment of that factor produces on the output of the commodity.

2.2.3   The Heckscher-Ohlin Theorem

The two-factor, two-good, two-country version of the Heckscher-Ohlin (HO) proposition states that each country exports the good that intensively uses its relatively abundant productive factor. (It also follows that in this model each country exports (embodied in goods) its relatively abundant factor and imports its relatively scarce factor.) To establish this relationship as a theorem, it is necessary to assume that in both countries there exists identical, constant returns-to-scale technology; identical, homothetic product preferences; different factor endowment ratios; perfectly competitive factor and product markets; perfect mobility of factors domestically but complete immobility internationally; and free trade. In addition factor-intensity reversals are ruled out.

The box and production-possibilities diagrams utilized in explaining the Stolper-Samuelson and Rybczynski theorems can also be used to explain the HO theorem. However, rather than assuming that the change in the size of a Stolper-Samuelson box represents a change in the quantities of the two factors available to a home country, as was done in explaining the Rybczynski theorem, we interpret a different-sized box as representing the quantities of the two

factors possessed by the other country (i.e., the foreign
country). With identical constant returns-to-scale production functions and identical homothetic preferences across
both countries, we can treat the addition of another country
with different capital and labor endowments as if the first
country's factor endowments have changed to these new
quantities.

Since the HO theorem depends only on differences in
relative factor endowments between two countries, we can
utilize a Stolper-Samuelson box diagram with the same absolute quantities of labor and capital as depicted in figure
2.3 in explaining the Rybczynski theorem. Let figure 2.5 be
such a diagram. The point O_2 indicates the quantities of
capital and labor available to the home country, and the
point O_2^* indicates the quantities of capital and labor available to the foreign country. Since the slope of the diagonal
line O_1O_2 is greater than the slope of the diagonal line

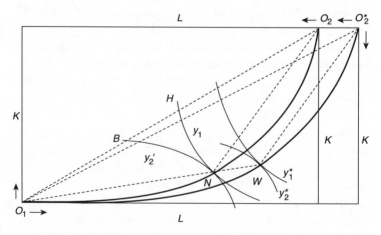

Figure 2.5 Two-country use of Stolper-Samuelson diagram

$O_1O_2^*$, the home country is assumed to have a higher endowment ratio of capital to labor than the foreign country. The Pareto efficiency locus for the home and foreign countries are represented by the curves O_1NO_2 and $O_1WO_2^*$, respectively, in figure 2.5.[14]

Suppose that the point N in figure 2.5 indicates the home country's equilibrium allocation of its capital and labor supplies between the production of goods 1 and 2 under autarky conditions. At the point N the capital/labor ratio used in producing good 1 is indicated by the slope of the line O_1N (measured from its origin at O_1), while the higher capital/labor ratio utilized by the home country in producing good 2 is indicated by the slope of the line O_2N (measured from its origin at O_2). The outputs of goods 1 and 2 for the home country at point N in figure 2.5 are represented in figure 2.6 as the point N on the home country's production possibilities curve PNP', and a home-country's social or community indifference curve is tangent to the production possibilities curve at N. The price of good 1 in terms of good 2 under autarky conditions is indicated by (minus) the slope of the price line p_1/p_2, which is also tangent to the home country's production possibilities curve at N. The slope of the line ONS indicates the ratio of the home country production of good 2 to the production of good 1, y_2/y_1, under autarky conditions. It should be noted that due to the assumption of identical, homothetic preferences for the two countries, the community indifference curves of both countries have the same slope when they intersect with constant y_2/y_1 consumption-ratio lines, such as ONS.

The foreign country's production-possibilities curve is represented in figure 2.6 as the curve P^*SRWP^{**}. As was explained when discussing the Rybczynski theorem, the point W on this production-possibilities curve has the same

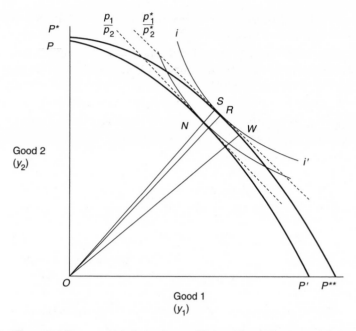

Figure 2.6 Two-countries' autarky equilibria with production-possibilities curves

slope as the point N on the home country's production possibilities curve. Moreover, because the slope of the foreign country's production possibilities curve at point S is less than its slope at point W, the slope of the foreign country's production possibilities curve at S is less than the slope of the home country production frontier at N. Also, because the ratio of the production of good 2 to the production of good 1 is the same at the points S and N, the slope of a community indifference curve (not shown) passing through the point S on the foreign country's production possibilities curve is the same as the slope of the home country's community indifference curve passing through point N and tangent to the home country's production possibility curve at that point. It follows therefore that a community indifference curve will be tangent to the foreign country's production possibilities frontier at a point to the southeast of S but northwest of W, namely at point R. Consequently the foreign country's autarky price ratio of good 1 in terms of good 2 p_1^*/p_2^* is lower than the home country's autarky price ratio for these goods so that the foreign country exports good 1 and the home country exports good 2 when free trade is opened between the countries. Thus, in accordance with the HO theorem, the home country, which is relatively capital abundant compared to the foreign country, exports the good that uses capital relatively intensively (good 2) and imports the good that uses labor intensively from the foreign country (good 1).[15]

It should be noted that this proof of the HO proposition does not depend on assuming, as in figures 2.5 and 2.6, that the factor endowments of the home and foreign countries differs only in that the foreign country has a greater supply of labor. Since the two countries are assumed to possess identical constant returns-to-scale production functions and identical homothetic preferences, it is apparent from the generalization of the Rybcynski theorem described in the preceding subsection that the production ratio of good 2 (the capital-intensive good) to good 1 for the foreign country will be less than the production ratio of good 2 to good 1 for the home country at all points where the slopes of the two production possibilities curves are the same. Thus the slope of the home country's production possibilities curve at the good 2/good 1 production ratio at its autarky point (N) will be greater than the slope of the foreign production possibilities curve at the same good 2/good 1 production ratio (the slope of ONS in figure 2.6). This implies that the good 2/good 1 production ratio (the slope of OR) at the foreign country's autarky point (R) will be less than the good 2/good 1 production ratio at the home country autarky point. Therefore the home (capital) abundant) country exports good 2 (the capital-intensive good) and the foreign (labor abundant) country exports good 1 (the labor-intensive good).

When depicting the free trade equilibrium in a figure such as figure 2.6 (this is not shown since the curvatures of the home and foreign production possibilities curves and the common social indifference curves are not sufficient for the free trade production and consumption points for the two countries to be clearly distinguishable), the common price line under free trade conditions has a (minus) slope somewhere between (minus) the slope of the p_1/p_2 line in the diagram and (minus) the slope of the p_1^*/p_2^* line in the figure. The home country's production point in figure 2.6 is to the northwest of N on the home country's production possibilities curve, while the foreign country's free trade production point is somewhere between points R and W on its production frontier. The common ratio at which the two countries will consume both goods lies along a line from the origin O that passes between points N and R. The shapes of the community indifference curves and the production possibilities curves determine exactly the market-clearing relative prices, the level of trade, and the equilibrium levels of production and consumption.[16]

2.2.4 The Factor Price Equalization Theorem

Although Heckscher maintains in his 1919 article that free trade can equalize factor prices, Ohlin rejects this conclusion both in his 1924 PhD thesis and 1933 book. Instead, he argues that free trade merely *tends* to equalize factor prices.

But, as Samuelson (1948) points out, Ohlin's reasoning in reaching this conclusion is not very satisfactory, and he does not state which theoretical assumptions would be necessary for factor price equalization to occur. It was not until 30 years after Heckscher's article and 25 years after Ohlin's PhD thesis that Samuelson (1948, 1949) first rigorously proved that complete factor price equalization takes place under the standard assumptions of the two-good, two-factor, two-country model when both countries produce both goods. In his Foreword to the volume edited by Flam and Flanders (1991), which presents the English translations of Heckscher's 1919 article and Ohlin's 1924 PhD thesis, Samuelson remarks that it is a pity that Ohlin did not "descend from full generality to strong and manageable cases—such as two factors of production and two-or-more goods" (Flam and Flanders, 1991, p. ix). Ohlin would have, Samuelson continues, "really understood his own system had he played with graphical versions" and have avoided the fallacy that "regions with divergent endowments could not without contradiction generate exactly equal factor returns."[17]

Samuelson had, of course, "played with graphical versions" of Ohlin's model by modifying the Bowley-Edgeworth box diagram and using a graphical depiction of a country's production possibilities frontier in explaining the Stolper-Samuelson theorem. Indeed the factor price equalization relationship is evident in figures 2.5 and 2.6, which use both the box and production possibilities frontier diagrams to explain the HO theorem. Figure 2.7, which is based on figure 2.5, is used to show explicitly the factor price relationship.

Assume that in figure 2.7 the points N and Z on the Pareto efficiency loci, O_1FNO_2 and $O_1ZGO_2^*$, of the home and foreign countries, respectively, indicate the two countries'

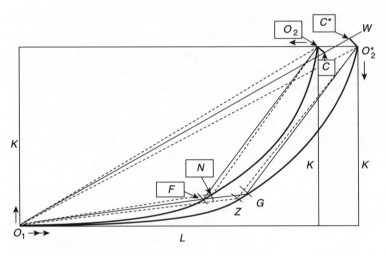

Figure 2.7 Factor price equalization under free trade

distributions of capital and labor at their autarky points. Since the home country is assumed to be relatively capital abundant compared to the foreign country and since tastes are assumed to be identical and homothetic for the two countries, the ratio of capital to labor used in producing the two goods under autarky conditions is greater in the home country than in the foreign country (the slopes of O_1N and O_1Z for good 1, respectively, and the slopes of O_2N and O_2^*Z for good 2, respectively). This also implies that the price of labor relative to the price of capital (the (minus) slopes of the tangencies between the two sets of isoquants (not shown) or the (minus) slopes of the short lines passing in a northwest direction through these points) is higher in the home country than in the foreign country. In turn this implies that the relative price of the labor-intensive good (good 1) is higher in the home country than in the foreign country under autarky conditions. Consequently, when trade between the two countries occurs, the home country imports good 1 and exports good 2 and the foreign country imports good 2 and exports good 1. Although goods 1 and 2 both embody capital and labor, the fact that the capital/labor ratio used in producing good 2 is greater than that used in producing good 1 implies that the home country exports capital and imports labor (and the foreign country exports labor and imports capital) under balanced trade conditions.

Next, assume that the point F on the home country's Pareto efficiency locus O_1FNO_2 and the point G on the foreign country's Pareto efficiency locus, $O_1ZGO_2^*$, indicate the distributions of capital and labor for the two countries under free trade production conditions. Since the prices of goods 1 and 2 are equal in both countries, we know from our assumptions on the production functions that the capital/labor ratio used in producing good 1 is the same in both countries, as is the capital/labor ratio used in producing good 2. The first ratio equals the slope of the line O_1FG, while the capital/labor ratio for good 2 equals the slopes of the parallel lines O_2F and O_2^*G (measured from O_2 and O_2^* as the respective origins of these lines). We also know from the assumption of identical, constant returns-to-scale production functions for goods 1 and 2 in both countries that the wages of labor are the same in both countries at points F and G as are the returns to capital at these points. Thus, factor price equalization is achieved in the two countries under free trade conditions when both commodities are produced.

Trade frees the consumption possibilities of a country from the constraints of its fixed factor endowments and, in effect, permits the country to consume endowments in a ratio different from its own endowments of the factors. With identical, homothetic preferences and both countries producing some of both goods under free trade, each country consumes the productive factors in a common proportion that equals the ratio of the combined capital and labor supplies of the two countries. In figure 2.7, where the capital supply is assumed to be the same in both countries, this ratio equals the slope of a line from O_1 that passes midway between the points O_2 and O_2^*, such as the line O_1CC^*W. The rate at which the two factors are exchanged equals the equilibrium wage/rental ratio or (minus) the common slopes of the two isoquant systems at the equilibrium production distributions of the two factors (points F and G). The home country trades from its endowment point O_2 to its consumptions point C by exporting good 2 and importing good 1, while the foreign country trades from its endowment point O_2^* to its consumption point C^* by exporting good 1 and importing good 2.

The best-known analyses concerning the likelihood of factor price equalization when the HO model is modified to include more than two goods and two factors are those of Dixit and Norman (1980) and Ethier (1984). One of their conclusions is that factor price equalization is unlikely in a world of more factors than goods. The well-known Ricardo-Viner model with two goods and two domestically mobile factors plus one immobile factor is an example of such a model where factor price equalization does not occur under free trade. However, when there are more goods than factors, equalization of factor prices across countries is not only possible but likely between countries with similar relative factor endowments.

2.3   The Heckscher-Ohlin-Vanek (HOV) Model

While the simple HOS model permits strong statements to be made about the effects of trade on product and factor prices, as well as on output and consumption, its relevance to the real world is severely limited by the assumptions of only two goods and two factors. Melvin (1968) showed that extending the standard two-factor (capital and labor), two-good, two-country model by including three rather than just two goods leads to the indeterminacy of both production and trade if all three goods are produced.[18] Under these conditions a capital-abundant country relative to the rest of the world need not export the most capital-intensive of the three commodities, for example. Consequently Ohlin's statement quoted at the outset of the first chapter, namely that: "Commodities requiring for their production much of the former [relatively abundant factors of production] and little of the latter [relatively scarce factors] are exported in exchange for goods that call for factors in the opposite proportions," need not hold literally. However, as Melvin pointed out, under balanced trade conditions the HO proposition is vindicated if we focus on the bundle of factors embodied in a country's exports and imports rather than on the factor content of each individual good. The exports of a country that is capital abundant relative to the rest of the world does, for example, embody a higher capital/labor ratio than its imports.

Travis (1964, ch. 3)[19] and Vanek (1968) generalized this relationship to the many-good, many-factor case, again assuming the existence of such conditions as identical constant returns-to-scale production functions, identical homothetic preferences, no factor-intensity reversals, perfect competition, at least as many products as factors, and factor price equalization. The key relationship that can be derived under these assumptions is that the amount of a particular factor of production embodied (directly and indirectly) in the country's net trade of goods and services equals its endowment of this factor minus its share of world consumption multiplied by the world endowment of this factor.

Let F_k^i be the amount of any factor k (where $k = 1, \ldots, M$) embodied in the vector of net exports of any country i (where $i = 1, \ldots, T$) whose net exports of a good equal that country's production of the good minus its consumption of the good. Furthermore, let V_k^i be country i's endowment of this factor, V_k^w $(= \sum_{i=1}^{T} V_k^i)$ be the world endowment of the factor, and $s^i = (Y^i - B^i)/Y^w$ be country i's GNP, Y^i, less its trade balance, B^i, or its aggregate consumption expenditures, C^i, $(= Y^i - B^i)$ on goods and services divided by world GNP, Y^w. Since it is assumed that all income is spent on goods and services, Y^w is also equal to the world's aggregate consumption of goods and services, C^w. Thus s^i is equal to country i's share in world aggregate consumption, or C^i/C^w. If $B^i = 0$, s^i is simply the country's share of world GNP. The basic Hecksher-Ohlin-Vanek (HOV) relationship can be expressed as

$$F_k^i = V_k^i - s^i V_k^w. \tag{2.7}$$

The intuition behind this relationship is straightforward. First, since preferences are identical and homothetic in each country and since product prices are the same everywhere under free trade, the proportion of a country's total consumption expenditures spent on any particular good is the same for all countries. The differences in absolute amount spent on each commodity among the countries are simply proportional to the consumption levels among the countries. A country whose aggregate consumption spending is, for example, 10 percent higher than in another country consumes 10 percent more of all goods than the second country. Next, since identical, constant returns-to-scale production functions exist for each good in all countries, factor-intensity reversals are ruled out, and factor prices are equalized for all countries, it follows that under free trade equilibrium conditions, the amount of each factor used per unit of output of each good is the same for all countries. Thus countries not only consume goods in the same proportions, but they also consume the productive factors embodied in the goods in the same proportions, with the absolute amounts of spending on embodied factor services varying in proportion to the levels of consumption spending among the countries.

If a country's consumption level represents (say) 5 percent of the world's consumption level ($s^i = 5$ percent) the country consumes 5 percent of the world's supply of each factor of production. Consequently, a country whose endowment of a productive factor (V_k^i) is greater (less) than the country's consumption of the factor $(s^i V_k^w)$ becomes a net exporter (importer) of the factor (embodied in goods) to the extent of this difference: $F_k^i = V_k^i - s^i V_k^w$.

The Vanek relationship implies that the ordering (from highest to lowest) of the ratios of a country's net exports of its productive factors (embodied in trade) to the world endowments of these respective factors is the same as the ordering of the ratios of its endowments of these factors to the world endowments of these factors. For example, let F_H^i, F_K^i, and F_L^i be the amounts of human capital, physical capital, and unskilled labor, respectively, embodied in country i's net exports; let H^i, K^i, and L^i be the country's endowments of these factors; and let H^w, K^w, and L^w be the world endowments of these factors. Following the relationship specified in equation (2.7), the embodied trade in these particular factors can be related to the country's and the world's endowments of these factors in the following manner:

$$F_H^i = H^i - s^i H^w;$$ (2.8a)

$$F_K^i = K^i - s^i K^w;$$ (2.8b)

$$F_L^i = L^i - s^i L^w,$$ (2.8c)

where s_i is the country's share of world consumption. Dividing each equation by the world supply of the factor yields the equations

$$\frac{F_H^i}{H^w} = \frac{H^i}{H^w} - s^i,$$ (2.9a)

$$\frac{F_K^i}{K^w} = \frac{K^i}{K^w} - s^i,$$ (2.9b)

$$\frac{F_L^i}{L^w} = \frac{L^i}{L^w} - s^i.$$ (2.9c)

It follows that if $H^i/H^w > K^i/K^w > L^i/L^w$, then $F_H^i/H^w > F_K^i/K^w > F_L^i/L^w$. In other words, the ordering of the ratios of a country's endowment of each factor to the world endowment of the factor is the same as the ordering of the trade in each factor to the world endowment of the factor. This relationship implies that the HO proposition holds: countries export their relatively abundant factors and import their relatively scarce factors.

It should also be noted that this latter ordering relationship between a country's endowments of factors and its net exports of factors still holds even if there is a uniform productivity differential between the country's productive factors and those of the rest of the world. Let the home country be numbered 1 and the rest of the world be numbered 2, and let there be two factors, physical capital K and labor L. Equation (2.9) for capital and labor for country 1 can be expressed as

$$\frac{F_K^1}{K^1 + K^2} = \frac{K^1}{K^1 + K^2} - s^1 = \frac{1}{1 + K^2/K^1} - s^1, \qquad (2.10a)$$

$$\frac{F_L^i}{L^1 + L^2} = \frac{L^1}{L^1 + L^2} - s^1 = \frac{1}{1 + L^2/L^1} - s^1, \qquad (2.10b)$$

where country 1's endowments of the two factors are K^1 and L^1, the endowments of the other countries of the world are K^2 and L^2, and the world endowments of the two factors in this two-country model K^w and L^w, equal $K^1 + K^2$ and $L^1 + L^2$, respectively. Assuming that the ratio of country 1's endowment of physical capital to the world endowment of physical capital is greater than the ratio of country 1's endowment of labor to the world endowment of labor or that $K^1/(K^1 + K^2) > L^1/(L^1 + L^2)$, the following relationship holds:

$$\frac{1}{1 + K^2/K^1} > \frac{1}{1 + L^2/L^1}. \qquad (2.11)$$

Now suppose that δ is the ratio of the productivity of the rest of the world's capital and labor (country 2's capital and labor in this case) relative to the productivity of country 1's capital and labor. Moreover, assume that δ is less than unity. Expressing the world endowments of capital and labor in productivity equivalent units, the following relationship holds, since the productivity coefficient is the same for both productive factors:

$$\frac{F_K^1}{K^1 + \delta K^2} = \frac{K^1}{K^1 + \delta K^2} - s^1 = \frac{1}{1 + \delta K^2/K^1} - s^1, \qquad (2.12a)$$

$$\frac{F_L^1}{L^1 + \delta L^2} = \frac{L^1}{L^1 + \delta L^i} - s^1 = \frac{1}{1 + \delta L^2/L^1} - s^1, \qquad (2.12b)$$

where s^1 is country 1's new share of world consumption.

Since equation (2.11) holds by assumption, we have the following:

$$\frac{1}{1 + \delta K^2/K^1} > \frac{1}{1 + \delta L^2/L^1}. \qquad (2.13)$$

Thus the ordering of the endowment relationships and the ordering of trade in the two factors does not change by introducing a uniform productivity factor. These relationships also do not change if there are more than two factors. Although factor price equalization between the country and the rest of the world is achieved under these conditions in terms of efficiency units of each factor, it does not exist in terms of the nominal units of the factors.

Staiger, Deardorff, and Stern (1987) and Brecher and Choudhri (1988) formulate and then test a country-pair version of the HOV model that has the considerable advantage of not requiring measurements of the supply of productive factors for the world as a whole (w). The basic HOV equations for two specific countries indexed by $i = 1, 2$ and their net exports of a particular factor, $k = K$ (capital), are

$$F_K^1 = K^1 - s^1 K^w, \qquad (2.14)$$

$$F_K^2 = K^2 - s^2 K^w. \qquad (2.15)$$

Combining equations (2.14) and (2.15) into one relationship and eliminating the unobserved world endowment of the factor yields the relationship derived by Staiger, Deardorff, and Stern (1987):

$$[F_K^1 - \alpha F_K^2] = [K^1 - \alpha K^2], \tag{2.16}$$

where $\alpha = s^1/s^2$.

If $s^1 = s^2$ implying that $\alpha = 1$, for example, and if the exports of the services of capital to the world by country 1 are greater than those of country 2 to the world, the endowment of capital in country 1 ought to be greater than the endowment of capital in country 2. In the case where expenditure shares in the two countries differ, α simply controls for the difference in country size and the same interpretation applies.

The Brecher-Chourdri (1988) version of a country-pair test is based on the relationship that, in the HOV model, the amount of any factor k embodied in a dollar of domestic expenditures must be the same for any two countries. First, let V_k^{Ci} be the amount of any factor k embodied in the aggregate consumption of any country i, using domestic input requirements. Thus

$$V_k^{Ci} = A_k^i D^i, \tag{2.17}$$

where D^i denotes a column vector of consumption flows of the N goods and services for country i and A_k^i is a corresponding row vector of direct and indirect requirements of factor k used in the production of goods of this country. Now assume that the HOV relationships hold for only two trading countries (country 1 and country 2) in a multicountry world. Since the two countries have the same constant returns-to-scale technology, identical homothetic tastes, perfect competition, free trade, and same factor prices, its follows that

$$A_k^i = A_k^2 \qquad \text{for all } k, \tag{2.18}$$

where A_k is a common vector of factor k's requirements for the two countries, and

$$D^1 = \beta D^2,\tag{2.19}$$

where D^1 and D^2 are column vectors of consumption flows for countries 1 and 2, respectively, and β is a scalar indicating the ratio of the consumption expenditures of country 1 on any product to the consumption expenditures of country 2 on this product. The following basic proposition for the two-country version is obtained by estimating the factor content of consumption from equation (2.17) and using equations (2.18) and (2.19),

$$V_k^{C1} = \beta V_k^{C2} \qquad \text{for all } k.\tag{2.20}$$

Since $\sum_{i=1}^{N} D' = C'$ and $\sum_{i=1}^{N} D^2 = C^2$ (where C^1 and C^2 represent aggregate consumption expenditures in countries 1 and 2), equation (2.20) can be written as

$$\frac{V_k^{C1}}{C^1} = \frac{V_k^{C2}}{C^2}.\tag{2.21}$$

In words, the amount of factor k embodied in a dollar of domestic aggregate expenditures must be the same for both countries. As the authors point out, this hypothesis can also be expressed in the form derived by Staiger, Deardorff, and Stern (1987).

2.4   The "New" Trade Theory and Differentiated Products

Two key assumptions of the standard HOV model are that all domestic and foreign firms in a particular industry produce a homogeneous product, and this product is produced under constant return-to-scale conditions. Consequently, with zero international transportation costs, a country will either export or import this product depending on its relative factor endowments.[20] There is, in other words, no intra-industry trade in this model. In fact, as Grubel and Lloyd (1975) demonstrated long ago, intra-industry trade is significant even at fine levels of industry classification. In 1996, for example, 57 percent of all US trade took place within industries classified at the four-digit level of the UN Standard International Trade Classification (Executive Office of the President 1998, p. 218). The development of the so-called new trade theory, which was pioneered in the late 1970s and 1980s by such authors as Krugman (1979), Lancaster (1980), Helpman (1981), and Helpman and Krugman (1985), was in part a response to the search for a formal theory to explain intra-industry trade. This section briefly describes the part of this theory that focuses on differentiated products and explains how it can be integrated into the standard HO framework.

The two basic assumptions of this approach are (1) there are industries in which products are differentiated and for which there is demand for a wide spectrum of varieties in each country, and (2) each variety of a differentiated product is produced with internal economies of scale. In this framework of Chamberlin-type monopolistic competition, equilibrium in such industries involves the production of a finite number of varieties in more than a single country, with each firm producing a different variety. Free entry ensures the elimination of profits.

To simplify the exposition of a model with these relationships, assume that each variety in a differentiated product sector is produced with the same increasing returns-to-scale production function and that factor proportions among the countries are sufficiently similar to achieve factor price equalization. Moreover assume that consumer preferences are identical and are of a love-of-variety type such that each consumer wants to purchase a certain amount of each variety of the differentiated product. Consequently, in a trading equilibrium, countries export a portion of their unique varieties and import portions of the sector's unique varieties produced by other countries.

Other key economic variables such as the equilibrium factor proportions used by the trading countries in producing both differentiated and homogeneous products and net exports or imports of these products are determined by relative factor proportions, tastes, and technology in the same way as in the standard HOV model. Thus *inter-industry* trade is determined by comparative advantage based on differences in relative factor endowments, and *intra-industry* trade is the result of the existence of industry-level increasing returns. One important prediction of the model supported by the data on trade among countries is that the relative importance of intra-industry trade compared to inter-industry trade increases as countries become more similar with regards to relative factor endowments.

2.5   The Helpman Non–Factor Price Equalization Model

Although most of the theoretical analysis in trade theory that has developed since the publication of Ohlin's book in 1933 assumes factor price equalization under free and costless trade, some authors have investigated what predictions can be made about the factor content of trade in the absence of factor price equalization and assumptions on preferences. Helpman (1984a), who extends the analyses of Brecher and Choudhri (1982b) and of Deardorff (1982), is a notable example. Like Ohlin (1933, app. 1), Helpman assumes that countries have identical, constant returns-to-scale production functions and that they produce in separate cones of diversification. Thus factor prices are not equalized. He then derives the *bilateral* trade relationship that the flow of a factor embodied in trade should be toward the country with a higher price of the factor.

This prediction is easily explained with the aid of the Lerner diagram used by Helpman.[21] Figure 2.8 depicts combinations of capital and labor such that the quantity of any good, y_i, times the free trade price of the good, p_i (where $i = 1, \ldots, N$), equals one unit of revenue ($p_i y_i = 1$) for six different goods ($y_1 = 1/p_1, y_2 = 1/p_2, \ldots, y_6 = 1/p_6$). In

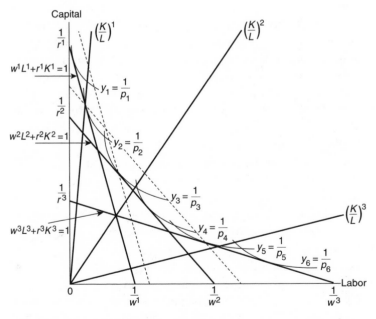

Figure 2.8 Helpman's bilateral trading relationships with non–factor price equalization

addition the capital/labor endowment ratios for each country i (where $i = 1, 2$, and 3) is indicated by the line $(K/L)^i$ drawn from the origin of the diagram, and the free trade wage/rental ratios for the countries are represented by the slopes of the unit isocost lines $w^i L^i + r^i K^i = 1$. Each unit isocost line is tangent to two of the unit-value isoquants. In the free trade equilibrium, country 1, which has the highest wage/rental ratio (as well as the highest capital/labor endowment ratio), produces goods 1 and 2; country 2, with the second highest wage/rental ratio (and second highest capital/labor ratio) produces goods 3 and 4; and country 3, with the lowest wage/rental ratio (and lowest capital/labor endowment ratio) produces goods 5 and 6. It is readily observable that the higher a country's capital/labor endowment ratio, the more capital and less labor it uses in all the goods it produces. Consequently, whatever the particular pattern of trade between *two* countries, the exports of the country with the higher capital/labor endowment ratio embody a higher capital/labor ratio than the exports of the country with a lower capital/labor endowment ratio. Thus the HO proposition holds for the pattern of bilateral trade between any countries in the absence of factor price equalization and any assumption regarding preferences.

It is useful to express this relationship using the value definition of relative factor abundance by comparing the actual cost of the productive factors embodied in a country's imports from another country and the hypothetical cost of these factors to the importing country at its own factor prices. In figure 2.8, the unit-value isoquants for the six goods each show the minimum combinations of capital and labor needed to produce one dollar's worth of each good at its free trade price, while the solid isocost lines tangent to these unit-value isoquants show the combinations of capital and labor that cost one dollar in the country producing the goods. The tangency points between the unit-value iso-quants and the one-dollar isocost lines indicate the combi-nations of capital and labor that yield the greatest quantities of goods that can be produced for $1. At these equilibrium points, one dollar spent on capital and labor in the country producing the good yields one dollar's worth of the good at its free trade price.

Consequently, if country 2 imports good 2 from country 1, the actual cost paid by country 2 for the capital and labor embodied in one dollar's worth of commodity 2 imported is obviously one dollar, the cost to country 1 of the quantities of capital and labor needed to produce this amount of the good at country 1's factor prices. Because of identical tech-nologies across countries, if these quantities of capital and labor are given to country 2 as an addition to its factor endowments, country 2 could clearly produce with these factors at least the value of its imports of commodity 2 from country 1. This can be seen by drawing a dashed isocost line parallel to country 2's unit cost line for optimally producing goods 3 and 4 $(w^2L^2 + r^2K^2 = 1)$ through the factor content point used by country 1 to produce good 2. Since this dashed isocost line will be above and to the right of country 2's one-dollar isocost line $(w^2L^2 + r^2K^2 = 1)$ that is tangent to the unit-value isoquants 3 and 4, the cost to country 2 of importing good 2 from country 1 is less than or equal to the cost to country 2 to produce good 2 at its own factor prices with the factor quantities used by country 1 to produce good 2 at country 1's factor prices.

This relationship can be generalized as

$$(w^j - w^i)F^{ij} \geq 0, \tag{2.22}$$

where w^j and w^i are the vectors of factor prices in any two countries, j and i (countries 2 and 1, respectively, in figure 2.8) and F^{ij} is the *gross import* vector of factor content of country j from country i measured with the technology matrix employed in the exporting country. Similarly, for the imports of country i from country j (goods 3 and 4 in figure 2.8),[22] the relationship can be expressed as

$$(w^i - w^j)F^{ji} \geq 0, \quad \text{or equivalently,} \tag{2.23}$$

$$(w^j - w^i)F^{ji} \leq 0. \tag{2.24}$$

Combining equations (2.22) and (2.24) yields the basic Helpman (1984a) relationship:

$$(w^j - w^i)(F^{ij} - F^{ji}) \geq 0, \tag{2.25}$$

which can be interpreted as stating that, on average, country j is a net importer from country i of productive factors (embodied in goods) that are cheaper in i than in j and country i is a net importer from country j of embodied factors that are cheaper in j than in i. As Helpman (1984a) proves, this relationship also implies that the factor content of exports from country i to j has, on average, a higher ratio of productive factors with which i is relatively well endowed than does the comparable ratio of exports from country j to i.

2.6   Ohlin on Modern Heckscher-Ohlin Trade Models

In the 35 years between the publication of Ohlin's book in 1933 and Vanek's article in 1968, mainstream trade theory evolved from an intuitive statement about the relationship between a country's relative factor endowments and the direction of its net trade in these factors into an elegant general equilibrium model that not only rigorously established this relationship but also set forth a number of other surprisingly strong yet simple theorems. This was a remarkable theoretical accomplishment. As a pioneer in advocating a general equilibrium approach to trade theory, Ohlin, who lived until 1979, must have been pleased with this formalization of his ideas. However, Ohlin believed that international trade theory should cover much more than the static implications for trade of differences among countries in relative factor endowments. He was very much aware of the unrealistic nature of his basic framework and devoted large parts of his analysis, particularly in this 1933 book, to exploring the implications of modifying this framework.

One of the key assumptions that he believed should be modified to develop a more realistic trade model was that of constant returns-to-scale production functions. He repeatedly stressed the importance of economies of scale as a determinant of the commodity structure of international trade, and in his 1924 thesis he explicitly listed "differences in endowments of productive factors" and "the limited divisibility of these factors, that is, the advantages of large-scale production" as the two causes of trade between regions (see Flam and Flanders 1991, p. 83).[23] Ohlin emphasized (e.g., see ch. 3, sec. 3) that sometimes the reason why one country exports a particular commodity to another country when trade between them is opened is because the domestic market for the good is larger in the first country under the no-trade conditions. If economies of scale are important over the range of the different production levels in the two countries, unit costs are lower in the first country for the same set of factor prices. Consequently this country exports the good when trade is opened between the two economies.

Ohlin also devoted considerable attention to exploring the implications of lifting such assumptions as the complete mobility of productive factors within countries and the complete immobility of factors among countries, fixed endowments of productive factors in each country, and qualitative differences among broadly similar factors of production. He argued, for example, for the use of location theory to help deal with the fact that within-country and between-country factor mobility is more a matter of a continuum rather than an all or nothing matter. Similarly he discussed how the opening of trade between countries results in price effects that not only affect movements of factors internationally but also the rates at which factor endowments change domestically. Furthermore Ohlin devoted considerable attention to discussing the effects of qualitative differences in productive factors such as labor. At one point (p. 94) he treated what would be regarded today as non-identical productions functions for the same product in two countries as simply different productive factors.[24]

Still another difference between his view of what topics international trade theory should cover and the nature of the HO models that have been developed since his 1933 book is the inclusion in Ohlin's framework of factors affecting trade patterns such as variations in the degree of economic stability among countries, differences in social conditions (e.g., the tax system), and the extent of monopolistic economic conditions. Finally, Ohlin strongly believed that international trade should be analyzed not simply in a static general equilibrium framework but one aimed at explaining the development of trade patterns over time.

Thus, although Ohlin must have been pleased with the adoption by trade theorists of his general equilibrium approach, he also must have been somewhat disappointed in their almost exclusive focus on discovering further implications that could be drawn from such simplifying assumptions as constant returns to scale and identical, homothetic preferences. In doing so, trade theorists followed their classical and neoclassical predecessors in assuming such underlying conditions as factor supplies, tastes, technology, and institutional conditions to be exogenously determined rather than attempting to provide a more rigorous theoretical framework for Ohlin's discussion of how changes in trade affected these basic conditions. As Ohlin's work indicates, it seems that he would have favored greater theoretical efforts in developing more dynamic models that moved trade theory toward greater realism and completeness to the theoretical refinements of his basic idea than actually took place.

3   Early Empirical Tests of the Heckscher-Ohlin Proposition

Economists involved in the early empirical investigations of the Heckscher-Ohlin proposition viewed the testing process rather differently than those who have undertaken empirical tests in more recent years.[1] Recent economists have rightfully stressed the need for any test to be informed by theory in the sense that the particular hypothesis being tested can be rigorously derived from the underlying theory. Early testers of the basic HO proposition, which states that countries export their relatively abundant factors and import their relative scarce factors, were very much aware that the assumptions needed for this proposition to hold in a rigorous theoretical sense, such as factor price equalization and identical preferences among countries, were patently false. Their investigations were aimed at determining if the economic forces behind the proposition were sufficiently strong that it would hold in the real world where the various underlying assumptions were at best just tendencies. However, in doing so, they were not sufficiently careful in ensuring that their particular statistical tests were definitive as to whether the hypothesis did or did not hold.

3.1 Factor-Content Tests

The factor-content version of Heckscher-Ohlin models has been the basis of most of the empirical tests of the theory. The first and most famous test of this nature was undertaken by Wassily Leontief (1953), who utilized the input–output table that he had developed for the United States to estimate the amount of capital and labor used both directly and indirectly to produce a representative $1 million bundle of US exports and import replacements in 1947. Interestingly Leontief did not mention either Heckscher or Ohlin in his pioneering paper, probably because he was presenting the paper before a group of noneconomists (the paper was published in the *Proceedings of the American Philosophical Society*) and he wanted to emphasize to this group the importance of his input–output framework for understanding the productive structure of the US economy. He simply stated:

A widely shared view of the nature of the trade between the U.S. and the rest of the world is derived from what appears to be a common sense assumption that this country has a comparative advantage in the production of commodities which require for their manufacture large quantities of capital and relatively small amounts of labor. . . . Since the U.S. possesses a relatively large amount of capital—so the oft repeated argument goes—and a comparatively small amount of labor, direct domestic production of such "labor intensive" products would be uneconomical; we can much more advantageously obtain them from abroad in exchange for our capital intensive products. (pp. 332–33)

Leontief began his study by accepting the relative abundance of capital to labor in the United States as an empirical observation that "can hardly be refuted" (p. 343). He then compared the capital and labor content of a representative million dollars worth of US exports with the capital and labor content of a representative million dollars worth of imports using the US capital and labor requirements for both sets of goods. He pointed out that for this procedure to be proper for determining if there exists a comparative surplus of capital and scarcity of labor in the United States, the relative productivity of capital and labor, industry by industry, must be either the same in this country and the rest of the world or differ only by a constant proportion. Thus he made a key assumption of the simple Heckscher-Ohlin model.

Unexpectedly, Leontief found that the capital/labor ratio embodied in a representative per million dollar bundle of US exports was less than a representative per million dollar bundle of US import replacements. Specifically, he found that the amount of capital per worker embodied directly and indirectly in producing a million dollars of gross exports in 1947 was $13,991, whereas the amount of capital per worker embodied in a million dollars of gross import replacements in 1947 was $18,184. This ordering relationship has become known as the Leontief paradox. His calculations indicated both that the amount of capital embodied in a million dollars of import replacements was greater than that embodied in a million dollars of exports and that the human-years of labor embodied in a million dollars of exports were greater than that embodied in a million dollars of imports.

As the analytical explanation for his empirical results, Leontief suggested that American entrepreneurship and superior organization have raised the productivity of US labor more than capital and, as a result, US labor was sufficiently more productive than foreign labor in efficiency-unit terms to actually make the United States relatively abundant in labor compared to capital. He pointed out that if US labor were three times more productive than foreign labor, the endowment of capital per worker (measured in efficiency units) would be lower in the United States than many other countries so that the United States would, in effect, be a labor-abundant country.

As might be expected, Leontief's results stimulated similar studies for different countries and different years for the United States. Some conformed to expectations, while others did not. In a follow-up study based on 1951 (rather than 1947) trade data for the United States, Leontief (1956) again found that the capital/labor ratio embodied in imports was greater than that embodied in exports, as did Baldwin (1971, 1979) for US trade in 1962 and again in 1969. However, studies by Tatemoto and Ichimura (1959) of Japanese trade, Roskamp (1963) and Roskamp and Mc-Meekin (1968) of West German trade, and Bharadwaj and Bhagwati (1967) of Indian trade produced mixed results in terms of the apparent consistency of trading patterns with the factor proportions theory.

Most of these and other early studies that followed Leontief's 1953 article attempt to account for his unexpected results by adding additional factors of production to his two-factor framework.[2] For example, Vanek (1963) argued that introducing natural resources as a third factor of production and taking into account its complementarity with capital could explain Leontief's seemingly paradoxical findings. As he stated (1963, p. 135), "It may well be capital is actually a relatively abundant factor in the U.S. Yet relatively less of its productive services is exported than would be needed for replacing our imports because resources, which are our scarce factor, can enter productive processes efficiently only in conjunction with large amounts of capital." However, as Travis (1964, pp. 94–98) points out and

Vanek (1968) himself later proved rigorously, this explanation is inconsistent with the generalized Heckscher-Ohlin model, which is usually distinguished today from the simple two-factor model by adding Vanek's name to those of Heckscher and Ohlin (and dropping Samuelson's). Even though there are other general or specific factors besides labor and capital, it follows from the HOV theorem that under balanced trade conditions a capital-abundant country (relative to the rest of the world) exports capital (embodied in its goods) on a net basis and imports labor.[3]

A number of authors have investigated the implications of subdividing the aggregate labor used in Leontief's test into labor groups possessing different levels of skill and education. Kravis (1956) first pointed out that US export industries employed more highly skilled labor than did US import-competing industries. Keesing (1965, 1967), Kenen (1965), and Yahr (1968) provided further evidence concerning the empirical importance of different relative supplies of labor skills for explaining US as well as other countries' trade patterns. Kenen (1965) estimated the value of human capital involved in US export- and import-competing production by capitalizing the wage premium earned by various types of skilled labor over unskilled workers. Interestingly, when he estimated human capital by discounting at a rate of less than 12.7 percent and added this figure to Leontief's physical capital estimates, the paradox is reversed for 1947. However, as Kenen and others have pointed out, the influence of labor market imperfections due to economic and social factors make this capitalization procedure questionable for obtaining accurate measures of human capital. Furthermore, the assumption that capital moves freely between physical goods and human agents of production in the long run seems questionable. Baldwin

(1971) also pointed out the importance of human capital in explaining US trade by showing that the direct and indirect average years of education per worker and the direct and indirect average cost of education per worker were higher in US export than import-competing industries.

Another relationship that the generation of economists who followed Leontief considered as an explanation for his findings is the existence of factor-intensity reversals within relevant ranges of factor prices. Under these circumstances the nature of technology may be such that a country's exports to the rest of the world and the rest of the world's exports to that country may be either both capital intensive or both labor intensive. Then the Heckscher-Ohlin theorem cannot possibly be true for both countries. A study by Minhas (1963) seemed to indicate that factor-intensity crossovers were in fact extensive. However, subsequent analysis by Leontief (1964), using additional data provided by Minhas, found extremely little evidence of factor-intensity reversals within the relevant range of factor price ratios.

Other possible explanations for Leontief's findings that were investigated empirically by economists writing in this early period are the existence of nonidentical production functions across countries, economies of scale rather than constant returns to scale, nonidentical and/or nonhomogeneous preferences, and trade-distorting measures such as tariffs and subsidies. Each of these conditions is capable of explaining why a capital-abundant country might export labor-intensive rather than capital-intensive products.

A technology-based relative productivity advantage in labor-intensive compared with capital-intensive products could, for example, more than offset the tendency for a capital-abundant country to have a comparative advantage in capital-intensive goods. Proxies widely used by empirical trade economists of this period to measure the importance of the technology factor across industries were the proportion of expenditures on research and development (R&D) and the share of engineers and scientists in an industry's workforce. Keesing (1967), Gruber and Vernon (1970), and others discovered a strong positive correlation between the relative importance of R&D activities in American industries and the exports of these industries as a proportion of the total exports of all trading countries. These types of results are consistent with the theories of such economists as Posner (1961) and Vernon (1966), who maintained that the United States has enjoyed a technological advantage over its trading partners in some products due to the country's relatively high R&D efforts.

The importance of scale economies as a basis for the product pattern of US trade also received empirical support in early tests, especially by Hufbauer (1970), although the measures of scale economies were quite crude. However, researchers failed to find strong empirical support for preference differences between the United States and the rest of the world or government-imposed trade-distorting measures as a cause of the Leontief results.

Travis (1964) maintained that protection (broadly interpreted to include export subsidies) was "the most plausible of the theoretically and empirically possible explanations of the Leontief paradox" (p. 171). A key reason for this conclusion was his belief that the extent of the failure of assumptions of the HO model to hold in the real world, other than the assumption of free trade, was not sufficiently significant to result in Leontief's paradoxical findings. However, the evidence he cited to support this view, especially the evidence that production functions were identical across countries, seems weak. Moreover his case that the protection is the reason for Leontief's results is based mainly on an arithmetic example plus his intuition that there is no other plausible possibility. In his review of Travis's book, Bela Balassa (1965) also expresses considerable skepticism about the conclusion of Travis that protection is the main reason for the poor empirical performance of the HO model.[4]

3.2   Methodological Criticisms of the Early Factor-Content Tests

Two major criticisms have been made of the early Leontief-type test of the Heckscher-Ohlin model. They are (1) the test may not correctly determine whether a country is capital abundant or labor abundant if the country's exports and imports are so unequal in value terms that the country is either exporting or importing both capital and labor and (2) the tests are incomplete because they usually have not involved an independent measurement of a country's factor endowments relative to the rest of the world.

3.2.1   Leamer on the Leontief Test

In a highly creative paper, Leamer (1980) was the first to point out that it is inappropriate, in general, just to compare the capital and labor content of a representative bundle of total exports and imports without also taking into account the balance of trade. In particular, he used a two-factor model in which a capital-abundant country runs a sufficiently large trade surplus with the rest of the world that, on balance, the country exports both labor and capital (embodied in its exports and imports of goods) to show it is possible for its imports of commodities to be more capital intensive than its exports. Leamer pointed out that the

United States did in fact export both labor and capital on balance in the year used by Leontief for his test. Moreover he proved that in this situation the proper test is to compare whether the capital/labor ratio embodied in *net* exports is greater or less than the capital/labor ratio embodied in its consumption as opposed to comparing whether the capital/labor ratio embodied in a country's exports is greater or less than the capital/labor ratio embodied in its imports. A country that exports both capital and labor is revealed to be capital abundant if the ratio of its net exports of capital to its net exports of labor is greater than the ratio of its total consumption of capital to its total consumption of labor. He also established that a country is revealed to be capital abundant regardless of whether its trade is balanced if the ratio of the capital embodied in production to the labor embodied in production is greater than its ratio of the consumption of capital to the consumption of labor.

Leamer then proceeded to show that these two tests were actually satisfied in 1947, even though the ratio of the capital to labor embodied in a representative bundle of exports was less than the ratio of capital to labor embodied in a representative bundle of imports.[5] Thus he showed that the United States was revealed to be capital abundant in 1947, and that Leontief's paradoxical result for that year was resolved.

Leamer's point about the inappropriate nature of Leontief's test of the Heckscher-Ohlin proposition can be shown by expressing the basic Vanek relationship for country i for the two factors, capital K and labor L, as

$$F_K^i = K^i - s^i K^w,\tag{3.1a}$$

$$F_L^i = L^i - s^i L^w \tag{3.1b}$$

(e.g., see equations 2.8b and 2.8c), where $F_K^i(F_L^i)$ is the amount of capital (labor) embodied in the net exports of any country i, $K^i(L^i)$ is country i's endowment of capital (labor), $K^w(L^w)$ is the world endowment of capital (labor), and $s^i = (Y^i - B^i)/Y^w$ is country i's GNP, Y^i, less its trade balance, B^i or its aggregate consumption expenditures, C^i $(= Y^i - B^i)$, on goods and services divided by world GNP, Y^w.

Now rewrite equations (3.1a) and (3.1b) as

$$K^w = \frac{K^i - F_K^i}{s^i},$$ (3.2a)

$$L^w = \frac{L^i - F_L^i}{s^i}.$$ (3.2b)

Then, dividing both sides of equation (3.2a) by K^i and both sides of equation (3.2b) by L^i and rearranging terms yields

$$\frac{K^i}{K^w} = \frac{s^i K^i}{K^i - F_K^i},$$ (3.3a)

$$\frac{L^i}{L^w} = \frac{s^i L^i}{L^i - F_L^i}.$$ (3.3b)

By definition, country i is relatively capital (labor) abundant if K^i/K^w is greater (less) than (L^i/L^w) or, equivalently, K^i/L^i is greater (less) than K^w/L^w. It follows that country i is revealed by trade to be capital abundant, meaning $K^i/K^w > L^i/L^w$, if and only if

$$\frac{K^i}{K^i - F_K^i} > \frac{L^i}{L^i - F_L^i}.$$ (3.4)

If F_K^i is positive and F_L^i is negative, equation (3.4) clearly holds, and the country is thus revealed to be relatively capital abundant. Likewise, if F_K^i is negative and F_L^i is positive, the inequality sign in equation (3.4) is reversed, and the country is revealed to be relatively labor abundant. However, if both F_K^i and F_L^i are positive or both are negative (relationships that are quite possible if the value of gross exports are either considerably larger or smaller than the value of gross imports), the left-hand side of equation (3.4) could be either greater or less than the right-hand side, and therefore no inference can be drawn concerning whether the country is capital or labor abundant based on these sign patterns of net exports of capital and labor.

Rather than focusing on a country's net exports of capital and labor, meaning F_K^i and F_L^i, Leontief and other early testers of the HOS model compared the capital/labor ratio embodied in a country's *gross* exports with the capital/labor ratio embodied in its *gross* imports. As previously noted, they concluded that if the capital/labor ratio embodied in *gross* exports is greater (less) than the capital/labor ratio embodied in *gross* imports, the country is capital (labor) abundant. Letting K_x^i and K_m^i represent the capital embodied in country i's gross exports and gross imports, respectively, and L_x^i and L_m^i represents the labor embodied in these exports and imports, respectively, net and gross exports of capital and labor are related as follows: $F_K^i = K_x^i - K_m^i$ and $F_L^i = L_x^i - L_m^i$. Since $F_K^i > 0$ and $F_L^i < 0$ imply $K_x^i/L_x^i > K_m^i/L_m^i$, the comparison between net exports of capital and labor and the comparison between the ratio of gross capital exports to gross labor exports and the ratio of gross capital imports to gross labor imports both reveal the same relative factor abundance when this sign pattern of net exports of capital and labor holds: that is to say, they reveal that the country is relatively capital abundant. The two comparisons also reveal the same relative factor abundance if $F_K^i < 0$ and $F_L^i > 0$: that is to say, they reveal that the country is relatively labor abundant. (If trade is balanced, one or the other of these two conditions must exist.) But Leontief and the other early researchers failed to recognize that $K_x^i/L_x^i > K_m^i/L_m^i$ does not necessarily imply that $F_K^i > 0$ and $F_L^i < 0$ (or that $K_x^i/L_x^i < K_m^i/L_m^i$ necessarily implies that $F_K^i < 0$ and $F_L^i > 0$). Either of these relationships between *gross* capital/labor exports and *gross* capital/labor imports can hold even if F_K^i and F_L^i are both positive or both negative. Thus one cannot make any definite inference about relative capital abundance from comparing K_x^i/L_x^i and K_m^i/L_m^i unless F_K^i and F_L^i have different signs.

The left- and right-hand side denominators in equation (3.4), $K^i - F_K^i$ and $L^i - F_L^i$, respectively, are simply the quantities of capital and labor consumed by country i, K^{Ci} and L^{Ci}. Consequently, by substitution and rearrangement, equation (3.4) can be rewritten as

$$\frac{K^i}{L^i} > \frac{K^{Ci}}{L^{Ci}}. \tag{3.5}$$

This states that a country is revealed to be capital abundant if its production is more capital intensive than is its consumption. In addition equation (3.4) can be written as

$$-K^i F_L^i > -L^i F_K^i. \tag{3.6}$$

If F_L^i is positive, this can be expressed as $F_K^i/F_L^i > K^i/L^i$. Thus, when the country is a net exporter of both labor and capital, the country is capital abundant if net trade is more capital intensive than production. The opposite applies if F_L^i is negative.

In the quotation from Ohlin (1933) cited in the third paragraph of the introductory chapter, Ohlin stated that the commodities exported are in exchange for commodities imported. He did not discuss the implications for his hypothesis that there exist goods that are imported and exported as the result of income transfers due to grants or in return for claims on commodities produced in the future. In his mathematical appendix, for example, he explicitly assumed that there were no credit transactions and that exports balance imports. Apparently he thought that unbalanced trade would not affect his basic proposition.

While Leontief (1953) was well aware that US trade was not balanced in 1947 (he cited the export figure of $16.7 billion and import figure of $6.2),[6] he also apparently did not believe that it would affect the validity of his test of Ohlin's proposition. The same was true of other early testers of the Heckscher-Ohlin proposition.

Although Leamer was able to use Leontief's data to demonstrate that the pattern of US trade in 1947 was not inconsistent with the United States being a capital-abundant country relative to the rest of the world, he recognized that it was not possible to show this using Baldwin's (1971) findings for US trade in 1962, which confirmed the Leontief paradox in that year.[7] Moreover analyses undertaken by Maskus (1985) of the US trade and endowment structure for 1958 and 1972 still confirmed the Leontief paradox for both years under the testing procedures set forth by Leamer (1980).[8] Maskus (1985) described this as the "Leontief commonplace" in testing the HOV theorem for the United States and a 34-country world.[9] Davis and Weinstein (2001a) also note the existence of the Leontief paradox for the United States under the standard HOV model in their 1995 data set (see p. 1441). However, Trefler (1993) did not find the paradox in 1983 US data.

The data for the United States used by Bowen, Leamer, and Sveikauskas (1987) (hereafter BLS) in their multi-country, multi-factor test of the HOV theorem for 1967 also reveal the existence of the Leontief paradox using the test set forth by Leamer (1980). First, based on independent measures of the capital/labor ratio for the United States and the world as a whole, they find that the United States is abundant in capital relative to the world because K^{US}/L^{US} (= \$10,261) is greater than K^w/L^w (= \$5,310). However, their data also reveal the paradoxical result for a capital abundant country (see equation 3.5) that the US capital/labor endowment ratio is less than the US consumption ratio of capital to labor, namely that the difference between the two ratios is \$10,261 to \$10,288.

Surprisingly, BLS (1987, p. 796) maintained that there is no Leontief paradox revealed on the basis of their US data, "since the U.S. exports capital services but imports labor services, and this conforms to the ordering of U.S. shares of world capital (41 percent) and world labor (22 percent)." They obtained the result that the US exports capital and imports labor by first utilizing the relationship that s^i in the basic HOV equation, $F_k^i = V_k^i - s^i V_k^w$ (see equation 2.7), is equal to $(Y^i - B^i)/Y^w$ (where Y^i is country i's GNP, B^i is its trade balance, and Y^w is the world's gross product) so as to write this equation as

$$F_k^i = V_k^i - \frac{Y^i V_k^w}{Y^w} + \frac{B^i V_k^w}{Y^w}. \tag{3.7}$$

They then modified the equation by transferring the last term on the right-hand side to the left-hand side to obtain

$$F_k^i - \frac{B^i V_k^w}{Y^w} = V_k^i - \frac{Y^i V_k^w}{Y^w}, \tag{3.8}$$

where the left-hand side of this equation is expressed as F_k^{Ai} (the adjusted trade balance) and described as "the factor content if trade were balanced" (BLS, p. 794). BLS assumed that if trade had been balanced, net exports of the kth factor; that is, F_k^i, would have been less by an amount equal to the share of the trade balance in world income multiplied by the world supply of the factor. Consequently it is assumed that a country's spending of the trade balance on any two factors would be proportional to the world supplies of the two factors.

Obviously, if $F_k^i > 0$ but $F_k^i < (B^i V_k^w)/Y^w$, the left-hand side of equation (3.8) is negative while the left-hand side of equation (3.7) is positive. This is, in fact, what occurs with respect to US net trade in labor in the 1967 data used by BLS. The actual net trade in labor, F_L^{US}, in that year is +764,413 workers, while the ratio of the balance of payments surplus to world income multiplied by the world's labor supply, $(B^{US} L^w)/Y^w$, is +954,363. Thus the adjusted US trade balance for labor, F_L^{AUS}, is $-189,950$ workers. Expressing this number as a ratio of the US endowment of labor (as BLS did in their 1987 article) yields -0.25 percent. However, a similar adjustment to the actual US trade balance in capital, F_K^{US}, does not change the sign of F_K^{AUS} from that of F_K^{US}. The actual net US trade in capital in 1967 is +\$5.76 billion and the BLS adjustment, meaning $(B^{US} K^W)/Y^w$ is +\$5.11 billion. Consequently the BLS-adjusted trade balance is still positive at +\$651 million, and the ratio of this amount to the US endowment of capital is +.08 percent. Thus the authors were able to say that the ordering of the *adjusted* trade balance in capital and labor, or, a net export of capital and a net import of labor, corresponds to the ordering of the ratio of US capital supply to the world supply of capital (41 percent) and the ratio of US labor supply to the world labor supply (22 percent). Therefore they were able to state that there is no Leontief paradox in the US data for 1967.

In the NBER working paper version of their article (WP 1918) released in May 1986, BLS calculated the ratios of the *actual* US trade balances in capital and labor to the US endowments of capital and labor and compared the ordering of these ratios to the ratios of the US endowments of capital and labor to the world endowments of capital and labor.[10] The ratio of net US trade in capital in 1967 to the US endowment of capital, F_K^{US}/K^{US}, is 0.773 percent and the comparable figure for labor, F_L^{US}/L^{US}, is 0.998 percent. Thus, the ordering of these ratios indicates that the US exports a larger percentage of its labor supply than its capital supply, and consequently trade reveals the country to be relatively labor abundant. Because US capital is relatively more abundant in the US than is labor, from a world perspective of these endowments, the authors concluded in their working paper that the Leontief paradox holds for the United States in 1967.

BLS focused on the adjusted factor-content of net exports rather than on the actual factor-content of net exports on the grounds that this enabled them to utilize "a more appealing notion of factor abundance" (BLS 1987, p. 794n.).[11] The right-hand side of equation (3.8) is a measure of relative factor abundance that compares a country's endowment of any factor with its *income* share of world income multiplied by the world endowment of the factor. If this measure is positive (negative), the factor is defined as relatively abundant (scarce) on average compared to other resources. In contrast, when the HOV equation is expressed as $F_k^i = V_k^i - s^i V_k^w$ (equation 2.7) with the actual (unadjusted) trade balance on the left-hand side, the right-hand side, namely, $V_k^i - s^i V_k^w$ or $V_k^i - (C^i V_k^w)/Y^w$, becomes a measure of relative factor abundance that compares a country's endowment of a factor to its *consumption* share of world income multiplied by the world endowment of the factor.[12]

A more complete understanding of when and why a difference can arise between the sign patterns of the left- and right-hand sides of BLS's 1987 expression of the HOV relationship versus the left- and right-hand sides of their 1986 and Leamer's 1980 expression of the HOV relationship can be provided with the aid of figure 3.1. This depicts a country's endowments of capital and labor and indicates alternative possible consumption levels of these factors together with their associated trade levels. The capital/labor endowment and consumption ratios for the world are also indicated in the figure.

Let point E in the diagram represent the capital and labor endowments of country i. Assume that the country is capital abundant relative to labor, $K^i/K^w > L^i/L^w$ or $K^i/L^i > K^w/L^w$, where the slope of the line ORE equals the capital/labor ratio for the country and the slope of OC^1C^0 indicates the capital/labor endowment ratio for the world. Also assume that the country runs a trade surplus that is sufficiently large such that it exports both EK of capital and KC^1 of labor (embodied in goods). Its consumption of capital and labor is indicated by the point C^1.

First, suppose that the assumptions of the HOV model hold in the data and that the country consumes the two factors in the proportion in which they are consumed and

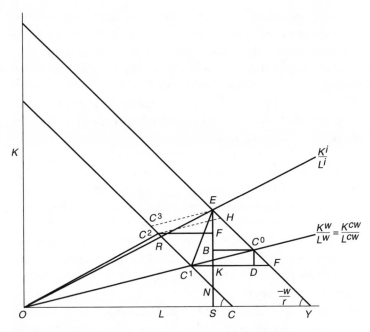

Figure 3.1 Leontief paradox and different definitions of relative factor abundance

supplied in the world as a whole, $K^{Ci}/L^{Ci} = K^{Cw}/L^{Cw} = K^{w}/L^{w}$. Thus, in figure 3.1, the point C^1 lies on the line OC^1C^0, whose slope is $K^{Cw}/L^{Cw} = K^{w}/L^{w}$. The slope of the trading line EC^1 equals the ratio of traded capital to traded labor or F^i_K/F^i_L. Consequently in this example $F^i_K/F^i_L > K^i/L^i > K^{Ci}/L^{Ci} = K^{w}/L^{w} = K^{Cw}/L^{Cw}$. Assume, in addition, that the angle, $-w/r$, is the equilibrium ratio of the wages of labor to the return on capital with OY and OC indicating the country's level of GDP and consumption, respectively, measured in units of labor. The balance of payments surplus equals YC ($= FC^1$) measured in units of labor and EN measured in units of capital.

Under the assumptions made by BLS, if trade were balanced, country i would spend the trade surplus on capital and labor in the proportion equal to the world capital/labor endowment ratio, K^w/L^w, or, in this example, on goods embodying DC^0 of capital and C^1D of labor. Thus its adjusted net trade in capital is its actual exports of capital, EK, minus the capital adjustment factor of DC^0 $(= KB)$ or net exports of EB of capital. Its adjusted net exports of labor are its actual exports of labor KC^1 minus the adjustment factor C^1D of labor or $-DK$ $(= -C^0B)$ of labor, that is, imports of labor equal to this amount. Since the country exports capital and imports labor on an adjusted basis, there is no Leontief paradox in terms of the sign test for this capital abundant country based on the BLS adjustment. EB of capital and BC^0 of labor are also the equilibrium volumes of exports of capital and imports of labor predicted under Leamer's basic HOV equation (2.7), namely $F_k^i = V_k^i - s^i V_k^w$ $= V_k^i - (C^i V_k^w)/Y^w$.

Next consider the case where the magnitude of the balance of payments surplus is the same, but country i's consumption point is C^2 in figure 3.1, which is a point that does not lie on the K^w/L^w line and thus does not satisfy the assumptions of the HOV model. In this case country i exports EF of capital and exports FC^2 of labor. The country is not only capital abundant, meaning $K^i/L^i > K^w/L^w$, but also exhibits such a home bias in its consumption of capital that its capital/labor consumption ratio, which is indicated by the slope of the line OC^2, is greater than the country's capital/labor ratio. On the basis of Leamer (1980), the Leontief paradox exists under these conditions.

Under the BLS adjustment assumption that the country spends the balance of trade surplus on capital and labor in the proportion K^w/L^w, the dashed line C^2H drawn parallel to the K^w/L^w line indicates how the country spends the surplus when trade is balanced. The point H indicates the hypothetical final consumption position on the GDP line EY under these conditions. Because H is below and to the right of the production point E on the GDP line, these adjustments mean that adjusted net exports of capital are positive and adjusted net exports of labor are negative. Therefore these adjustments eliminate the Leontief paradox. This is the case provided that the consumption point with the trade surplus lies on the line indicating possible consumption points between C^3 (the point from which a line parallel to OC^1C^0 and C^2H intersects the GDP line at E) and R (the point where the consumption line intersects the country's K^i/L^i line). If the consumption point with the trade surplus is above C^3 on the extension of the line CC^3, both Leamer (1980) and BLS (1987) indicate the existence of the Leontief paradox.

In algebraic terms, in a two-factor (capital and labor) model where a country is capital abundant and exports both capital and labor, the BLS adjustments to actual trade correctly reveal the country to be capital abundant if $K^{Ci}/L^{Ci} > K^i/L^i > F_K^i/F_L^i > K^w/L^w$. This ordering of a country's capital/labor consumption, its endowment, its trade ratio, and world-endowment ratios is the ordering that exists in the United States in 1967. In that year F_K^{US} (\$5.76 billion) > 0 and F_L^{US} (0.764 million workers) > 0 and K^{CUS}/L^{CUS} $(= \$10{,}288) > K^{US}/L^{US}$ $(= \$10{,}261) > F_K^{US}/F_L^{US}$ $(= \$7{,}537) > K^w/L^w$ $(= \$5{,}355)$. Consequently the authors were able to state that no Leontief paradox is evident in their adjusted trade figures for the United States.[13] However, since the US capital/labor endowment ratio (\$10,261) is less than its capital/labor consumption ratio (\$10,288), the criteria applied by BLS (1986) and Leamer (1980) incorrectly indicate the country to be labor abundant.[14]

Since the BLS article, most empirical trade economists have preferred to compare a country's ratio of its endowment of a factor to the world endowment of the factor to the country's share of *consumption* in world income rather than its share of *income* in world income (e.g., Trefler 1993, 1995; Davis and Weinstein 2001a, 2003; Feenstra 2004). However, one cannot say that one definition of factor abundance is right and the other is wrong. Still, as Kohler (1991) argued, researchers presenting sign or rank-order test results should at least examine the robustness of the results to the use of the different measures of relative factor abundance. It seems preferable to me to follow the 1980 Leamer procedure of comparing actual measured net exports of a factor (the left-hand side of equation 2.7) to the net exports of the factor predicted by the HOV equation (the right-hand side of this equation) rather than adjusting measured net exports by a term that presumes an assumption of the HOV model holds in the actual data being tested.

3.2.2   Brecher and Choudhri on Leamer's Tests

Brecher and Choudhri (1982a) pointed out another seemingly paradoxical relationship with Leontief's 1947 results that is not eliminated despite using Leamer's (1980) testing procedures with the 1947 data. As the two authors show, Leontief's findings that the United States exported both capital and labor on balance in 1947 imply under the HOV model that US consumption per worker must be less than consumption per worker in the world as a whole, meaning $F_k^i > 0$ iff $C^i/L^i < C^w/L^w$. They then cited independent data indicating that per worker expenditures in the United States in 1947 are in fact much larger than per worker expenditures in the world.

The relationship that they pointed out can be established by noting that s^i in the basic HOV equation ($F_k^i = V_k^i - s^i V_k^w$) is the ratio of country i's aggregate consumption expenditures to world aggregate consumption expenditures, and thus this equation can be rewritten as

$$F_k^i = V_k^i - \left(\frac{C^i}{C^w}\right) V_k^w = V_k^i \left[1 - \left(\frac{C^i}{C^w}\right)\left(\frac{V_k^w}{V_k^i}\right)\right]. \tag{3.9}$$

If labor is the particular factor of interest, equation (3.9) can be written as

$$F_L^i = L^i - \left(\frac{C^i}{C^w}\right) L^w = L^i \left[1 - \left(\frac{C^i}{L^i}\right)\left(\frac{L^w}{C^w}\right)\right]. \tag{3.10}$$

Since $L^w/C^w = 1/(C^w/L^w)$, a country's net exports of labor, F_L^i, is positive only if its per capita consumption, C^i/L^i, is less than the world's per capita consumption, C^w/L^w.

3.2.3   The Lack of Independent Measures of Factor Endowments

As pointed out at the beginning of this section, another criticism of the early Leontief-type tests of the HOV model is that they did not include an independent measurement of capital and labor endowments. Critics Deardorff (1984), Leamer (1984), Maskus (1985), and others, have stressed the fact that the HO proposition involves a relationship among three variables, namely, trade, factor-input requirements, and factor endowments, whereas studies such as Leontief's used data on only the first two.[15] Leveling this criticism at Leontief seems somewhat gratuitous, since those making it do not claim that an independent measurement of the US capital/labor endowment ratio might have revealed a different relationship than the one on which Leontief based his reasoning, namely that the United States possessed a higher ratio of capital to labor than the rest of the world in 1947.

As indicated by the discussion of his findings (see Leontief 1953, pp. 343–44), Leontief was well aware that for his results to be considered unexpected or paradoxical would require that the United States to be capital abundant relative to the rest of the world. His conclusion on this matter was, he states, based on "an empirical observation" that "can hardly be disputed" (p. 343). Studies of the value of the capital stock per worker did not exist at that time for many countries, but Leontief was almost certainly aware of the estimates by Clark (1940, 1951). For the year 1939 Clark estimated capital per worker to be lower in the United States than in the Netherlands, but higher than in Norway. His 1932 to 1934 estimates for Great Britain also suggests that the US figure is somewhat less than Great Britain's in 1939. However, Clark (1951, ch. 14, sec. 3) estimated the capital stock per worker in many poor countries to be less than 10 percent of the figure for such countries as the United States and Great Britain. Consequently there was little reason for Leontief not to accept as an empirical observation that the United States was capital abundant relative to the rest of the world in 1947, particularly when the destruction of capital in Europe during World War II is taken into account.

It should also be noted that Leontief was only testing whether US exports were more capital intensive than US imports, while the Heckscher-Ohlin proposition is concerned with whether the United States is capital abundant relative to the rest of the world. He was not trying to compare the actual amounts of net capital and labor in a representative bundle of exports and imports with the amounts of capital and labor that the HOV model predicts to be in these bundles. In other words, he carried out a sign test of the theory.

Subsequently Bowen, who was one of Leamer's PhD students, was able to utilize much better data to make independent estimates of the capital stock per worker in the United States and the rest of the world (reported in Leamer 1984, app. B, and in the data appendix of Bowen, Leamer, and Sveikauskas 1987) for the period from 1958 to 1975. These estimates confirm the capital abundance of the United States relative to the rest of the world in 1958, 1966, and 1975, for example. Moreover the magnitude and persistence of the difference between the capital/labor ratio of the United States and the world as a whole indicate that this was almost certainly the case in 1947. Bowen's estimates of the capital/labor ratio for the United States are $7,358 for 1958, $10,261 for 1966, and $19,382 for 1975. His estimates for the world as a whole (58 countries for 1958 and 1975 and 27 countries for 1966) are $1,492 and $6,515 in 1958 and 1975, respectively, and $5,310 in 1966.[16]

3.3 Regression Analysis

Another technique employed in a number of the early post-Leontief investigations of the determinants of a country's structure of trade is regression analysis. Studies by Keesing (1965, 1966, 1967), Gruber and Vernon (1970), and Hufbauer (1970) that utilized the regression approach have already been mentioned. This methodology was not primarily aimed at testing the Heckscher-Ohlin theory but at assessing the relative importance of some of the variables other than capital and labor that various authors had suggested as important explanatory factors of a country's trading patterns. Baldwin (1971), for example, regressed not just the amounts of capital per worker required directly and indirectly to product a unit of an industry's output on adjusted net US exports[17] but also included such industry variables as the proportion of engineers and scientists (a proxy for R&D activities resulting in new and improved products in the industry), the proportions of workers in various other skills groups or with different levels of education by industry, and a measure of the importance of scale economies in industries. His findings confirmed the significance of highly educated individuals such as engineers and scientists and those with 13 or more years of education along with capital/labor requirements as explanatory factors of the industry pattern of US trade in the early 1960s.[18]

Branson and Monoyios (1977) provided more comprehensive information concerning the importance of human capital in explaining the commodity composition of US trade. Utilizing data from Hufbauer (1970), they calculated measures of human capital for US manufacturing industries by discounting (at 10 percent) the excess of the average wage in each industry over the 1963 median wage earned in the United States by a male with eight years of education or less and multiplying by employment in the industry. They then regressed these industry measures of human capital, physical capital, and labor for the 1963 US net exports by industry. The sign on the human capital variable is significantly positive and the signs on both physical capital and labor are significantly negative.

Regression analysis provides useful information about various forces influencing the pattern of a country's trade across industries, but it is flawed as a method of formally testing the formal HOV model (see Leamer and Bowen 1981; Aw 1983). Specifically, it is possible that with more than two factors the signs of the regression coefficients do not duplicate the signs of the corresponding measures of factor abundance.[19] Bowen and Sveikauskas (1992) estimated the likelihood of this outcome, in practice, by comparing the signs of regression coefficients calculated for various numbers of factor inputs for each of 35 countries and the signs of the true relative abundance of these factors. They concluded (see p. 21) that for broad aggregates of factors such as capital, labor, and land "significant regression coefficients almost invariably reflect revealed factor abundance."

3.4 Conclusions

The results from early tests attempting to find statistical support for the Heckscher-Ohlin proposition were disappointing. The most famous of these tests, namely Leontief's (1953) analysis of US trade for 1947, produced the paradoxical result for a country generally regarded as being capital abundant that the capital/labor ratio of a representative bundle of its exports was less than the capital/labor ratio of a representative bundle of its imports. Although Leamer (1980) was able to demonstrate that Leontief's paradoxical result was reversed when the US trade balance for 1947 was appropriately adjusted, Leamer's reversal of the Leontief paradox failed to hold for other years in the 1950s, 1960s, and 1970s when the US trade balance was adjusted in the manner he specified. Davis and Weinstein (2001b, p. 18), who later also obtained paradoxical results with 1995 trade-balance-adjusted US trade data, concluded that adjustments for trade imbalances "have typically had scant impact on the HOV results."

Leamer's research does, however, points to a serious deficiency in the testing efforts of this early period, namely a failure to establish close links between Heckscher-Ohllin trade theory and the empirical techniques used in testing the theory. For example, Leontief and others implementing his testing approach failed to recognize that if a capital-abundant country's trade surplus with the rest of the world was sufficiently large that, on balance, it exported both capital and labor (embodied in goods and services), it is theoretically possible for its imports to be more capital intensive than its exports. Similarly researchers who utilized multiple regression techniques to identify the importance of relative factor endowments and other variables in shaping trading patterns did not seem to realize that when there are more than two productive factors, it is possible for the signs of the regression coefficients not to duplicate the signs of the corresponding measures of factor abundance. It has also been pointed out that most of the studies of this period failed to use independent measures of relative factor endowments. Still another drawback of the early empirical studies was their heavy reliance on the relevant trade and other economic data of only a small sample of countries.

These various deficiencies of the early studies eventually led to time-consuming efforts by some researchers to assemble the data needed for empirical studies involving the factor content of trade for many countries and many productive factors. These researchers were also more willing to investigate if any empirically straightforward modifications in the assumptions of the basic Heckscher-Ohlin model could result in strong support for the importance of relative factor endowments in shaping trading patterns. This is the subject of chapter 4.

4   Multi-country, Multi-factor Tests

Some multi-country testing had already been undertaken during the early testing period covered in the preceding chapter. Hufbauer (1970), for example, analyzed trade in manufactured goods of 24 countries for 1965.[1] He found a rank correlation coefficient of 0.70 between national fixed capital per person and capital embodied in national exports and a coefficient of 0.69 between the percent of professional and technical workers in the labor force of the various countries and the proportion of these types of workers embodied in their exports. Consequently he concluded that a combined physical capital and human skill theory "goes a long way to explain trade among manufactured goods" (Hufbauer 1970, p. 175).

4.1   Early Tests with Many Countries

Baldwin (1979) calculated the ratio of capital per worker in import-competing goods to capital per worker in export goods for 35 developed and developing countries for 1964 using, alternatively, US, EU, and Japanese labor and capital coefficients across industries as well as the input–output coefficients for these three countries. Capital per worker embodied in US import-competing goods for 1964 is not only again greater than in US export goods but also greater than unity for such industrialized countries as Germany, France, the United Kingdom, and Japan under all three sets of country coefficients. Another finding is that US and EU coefficients yield the same results concerning whether this ratio is above or below unity for 29 of the 35 countries,[2] whereas this relationship holds for only 21 countries in the comparison between US and Japanese coefficients.[3]

Leamer (1984) also investigated the role of relative factor endowments in accounting for trading patterns in a multi-country, multi-factor framework. Specifically, he regressed the net exports of each of 10 aggregate commodities on the supplies of 11 productive factors for 59 countries for the years 1958 and 1975. He found (1) that net exports of natural resource products such as petroleum and raw materials are positively related to supplies of such natural resources as coal, minerals, and oil; (2) that net exports of various crops are positively related to land endowments; and (3) that manufactured goods are positively related to capital and labor endowments. He concluded, consequently, "that the main currents of international trade are well understood in terms of the abundance of a remarkably limited list of resources. In that sense the Heckscher-Ohlin theory comes out looking rather well" (Leamer 1984, p. xvi).

4.2   The Bowen-Leamer-Sveikaukas (BLS) Test of the HOV Model

Bowen, Leamer, and Sveikauskas (1987; hereafter referred to as BLS) regard their study as the first rigorous, multi-country test of the HOV model. They calculated the amounts of each of twelve factors embodied in the "adjusted net exports" of 27 countries in 1967, using the US matrix of total input requirements for 1967. These were then compared to their independent measurements of the endowments of these factors in the 27 countries.

Their "adjusted net exports" of a factor, F_k^{Ai}, are equal to the actual net exports of the factor for a country minus the world endowment of the factor multiplied by the share of world income that the country's trade balance represents or $F_k^{Ai} = F_k^i - (V_k^w B^i / Y^w)$. As explained in section 3.2.1, comparing the sign of these "adjusted net exports" of a factor with the sign of the measure of relative factor abundance that they use can yield different results from comparing of the sign of actual net exports of a factor and the definition of relative factor abundance used by Leamer in his 1980 article and by BLS in their 1986 NBER working paper.[4] Fortunately, the differences produced with the two sign-matching procedures using the data reported by BLS in their data appendix do not change the overall conclusion about the sign results. BLS found a sign match for capital for 14 of their 27 country sample or 52 percent (see table 2 in their 1987 article), whereas the capital match using the procedure set forth in Leamer (1980; and followed by such later investigators as Trefler 1995 and Davis and Weinstein 2001a) yields a match of 16 of 26 or 59 percent. Similarly the number of sign matches for labor under the BLS procedure is 18 of 27 (67 percent). In contrast, the number of sign matches reported in BLS's 1986 NBER working paper is 15 of 27 for capital (56 percent) and 14 of 27 for labor (52 percent). Since one expects a 50 percent match just by chance, these results mean that there is "little support" (BLS 1987, p. 797) for the HOV hypothesis based on a sign test under either procedure.

An important feature of the BLS study is that these
authors attempted to improve upon their previous poor
results by utilizing regression analysis to compare the effects of modifying key assumptions of the model. One key
modification is that they regressed each country's measured
factor content of net exports on the predicted factor content
of net exports, where Hicks-neutral differences in technology, δ (and thus factor productivity), are permitted among
countries, though not among the factors within any country.
This modification changes the basic HOV relationship that
$F_k^i = V_k^i - s^i V_k^w$, where F_k^i, the content of factor k $(k = 1, \dots,$
$M)$ in country i's $(i = 1, \dots, T)$ net exports, is measured using US total factor requirements, V_k^i is the endowment of
factor k in country i, and $s^i V_k^w$ is the ratio of i's total consumption to world income, s^i, multiplied by the world endowment of factor k. The HOV equation now becomes
$F_k^i = \delta^i V_k^i - (s^i \sum_{i=1}^{T} \delta^i V_k^i)$, where δ is set equal to one for
the United States and equal to a country's ratio of factor
productivity compared to that of the United States for all
other countries. The term $\sum_{i=1}^{T} \delta^i V_k^i$ is the sum of all countries' supply of factor k expressed in efficiency units, or the
world supply of factor k expressed in efficiency units. A
country's relative productivity parameters are chosen to
minimize the sum of the squared residuals in the equation
$F_k^i = \delta^i V_k^i - (s^i \sum_{i=1}^{T} \delta^i V_k^i)$. The authors did not present any
theoretical reasons why productivity differences across
countries exist and pointed out in a footnote (BSL 1987,
p. 799) that the specification of neutral technological differences was chosen for tractability in estimation.

Although the hypothesis that the technology variable, δ^i
equals one for all countries can be rejected for all but three
of the 37 countries, the estimations do not produce sensible
results. Some of the estimated technology parameters are

greater than one, some are negative, and most are very different from unity.

Another modification tested by BLS is to replace the HOV assumption of identical, homothetic preferences for all individuals with the assumptions that all individuals have identical preferences with linear Engel curves[5] and that income is equally distributed within each country. Goodness-of-fit tests are utilized to judge the performance of this and other variations of the HOV model against the version in which neutral technological differences among countries are introduced or in which all the basic HOV assumptions are maintained. Their conclusion on this evaluation basis was that a model with neutral differences in factor input matrices and a measurement error in both trade and natural resource supplies performs best. However, this favored hypothesis does not produce "sensible estimates of many of the parameters" (BLS 1987, p. 803), especially estimates of the productivity parameters across countries.

It should be emphasized that the tests used by BLS to evaluate the performance of their various modified HOV models are quite different from the ones they used initially to judge how well the unmodified HOV model performs empirically. Their tests of the regression models are designed to determine which set of predictions of net factor exports most closely fits measured net factor exports. In contrast, their earlier sign tests are aimed at determining the extent to which countries export their relatively abundant factors and import their relatively scarce productive factors, namely the Heckscher-Ohlin proposition. An improved fit between measured and predicted net factor exports need not necessarily produce an increase in the number of sign matches between measured and predicted net factor exports.[6] Learning what types of modifications in the assumptions of the HOV model improve the fit of measured net exports regressed on predicted net exports is important for understanding why production and consumption levels differ across countries. However, BLS did not provide direct evidence about how well the basic Heckscher-Ohlin proposition performs. They did not report the results of sign tests for their various alternative hypotheses on an individual basis, but, in commenting on them as a group, the authors stated: "The Leontief-type sign and rank propositions, whether examined across countries or across factors, were generally not supported" (BLS 1987, p. 805). Their final conclusion is: "The Heckscher-Ohlin model does poorly, but we do not have anything that does better" (BLS 1987, p. 805).

4.3   Trefler's Tests and the Mystery of the Missing Trade

Trefler (1995) undertook the interesting exercise of comparing the actual quantities of measured net exports of a factor (the left-hand side of the HOV equation, F_k^i) and the predicted quantities of net exports of the factor (the right-hand side of the HOV equation, $V_k^i - s^i V_k^w$). In addition he performed the sign tests that had been undertaken by BLS. Since the BLS study showed that there is little more than a 50 percent chance that the signs of each side of the basic HOV equation match, Trefler did not expect the two sides of the equation to be equal in his test. However, he wanted to determine if there are systematic ways in which the test fails across countries and factors, and he collected data on trade and factor endowments for 1983 that cover 33 countries and 9 factors.

In performing the sign test of BLS, he did not use the "adjusted" net exports calculated by these authors. Instead, he measured the actual net exports of the factors for each country and compared them with the differences between the endowment of the factors and the country's consumption share of world factor endowments. Trefler found that the proportion of sign matches among the 33 countries and 9 factors is 50 percent, which implies "that the HOV prediction is about as good as a coin toss." Thus his analysis confirmed the conclusion of BLS that the Heckscher-Ohlin proposition performs poorly when confronted with relevant data for many countries.

Trefler described his key finding in comparing the volume of measured trade versus predicted trade under the HOV model as "the mystery of the missing trade."[7] Measured net exports are an order of magnitude smaller than predicted net exports: that is, measured trade is essentially zero when compared to predicted trade.[8] He also found that poor countries tend to be abundant in all factors (i.e., the ratio of a country's endowment of a factor to the world endowment of the factor is greater than the ratio of the country's consumption to world income), while rich countries tend to be scarce in most factors. Given the tendency for the ratio of measured to predicted trade to be compressed toward zero, the difference between actual and predicted factor trade becomes negative for poor countries and positive for rich countries. An obvious possible explanation for this relationship is that factors are less productive in the poor countries; that is, the factor endowments of poorer countries become smaller when expressed in productivity-equivalent units of a rich country such as the United States.

Trefler then tried to improve on the empirical performance of the HOV model both in terms of the sign test and the fit between the actual and predicted factor content of trade by modifying some of its assumptions with regard to technology and consumption. He introduced Hicks-neutral differences in productivity coefficients across countries under the restriction that there is a single coefficient for each country across all of its factors. In addition he allowed the neutral technological differences to differ between developed and developing countries. The first of these sets of estimates replicates one of the modifications to the Heckscher-Ohlin model tested by BLS. However, Trefler found that these authors incorrectly derived the appropriate estimation equation. With the proper equation, Trefler, unlike BLS, did not find an implausible set of neutral technological differences across countries, either for his 1983 data or for the 1967 data used by BLS. Instead, on the basis of the goodness of fit of this model[9] and the high correlation across countries between the neutral productivity factors and per capita income levels, he concluded that this model represents a significant improvement over the standard HOV model.[10] However, as he noted, his introduction of cross-country technological difference was instigated by the data and he did not present any theory about why there should be technology differences across countries (Trefler 1995, p. 1044).

As already noted, obtaining a good fit for the HOV quantitative relationship by introducing simple differences in factor productivity across countries does not necessarily mean that the Heckscher-Ohlin proposition concerning countries exporting their relatively abundant factors should also receive strong support. To determine the extent to which the Hecksher-Ohlin proposition holds after introducing such modifications of the HOV model, one needs to undertake such tests as comparing the signs of measured versus predicted factor trade, an exercise that BLS did not undertake with their modified factor trade predictions. Trefler re-

ported that with his 1983 data set the unweighted proportion of sign matches rises from 0.50 to 0.62 when the HOV
model is modified to permit Hicks-neutral technological difference among countries.[11] This latter proportion is still not
too much better than what one would expect from the flip
of a coin.[12] In short, in Trefler's data set, significantly improving the fit between measured and predicted trade is
not the same as significantly increasing support for the basic
Heckscher-Ohlin proposition. Introducing neutral productivity differences among countries accomplishes the first but
not the second goal. Moreover, if one's main objective is to
explain Trefler's missing trade, a key question with regard
to the productivity-differences explanation is why and how
these differences arise among countries.

Trefler also attempted to account for missing trade by
modifying the HOV model's assumption that countries consume all goods in the same proportion. Specifically, like
Armington (1969), he treated foreign goods as being different from domestic goods and used regression analysis of
the data to determine a country's consumption shares of
domestic versus foreign goods. This exercise essentially
involves measuring the extent of these differences under the
assumption that the missing trade is due entirely to preference differences between these two types of goods. Compared to the HOV theorem, the proportion of unweighted
sign matches increases from 50 to 62 percent, but the wide
variation among countries in the coefficients measuring
the relative preference for foreign goods (the coefficients for
the United States, Canada, and the Netherlands are 0.02,
0.38, and −0.41, respectively) raises questions about the
meaningfulness of the analysis.[13] However, combining the
Armington and neutral technology modifications increases
the proportion of unweighted sign matches to 72 percent.

4.4   The Davis-Weinstein Tests

The most comprehensive and systematic tests of the HOV model within a multi-country, multi-factor framework thus far are those by Davis and Weinstein (2001a–c). In their effort to improve the fit of the HOV model, these authors modified a broader set of the basic assumptions of this model compared to either BLS or Trefler, in part because of the availability of new standardized input–output tables for ten OECD countries. A drawback of their data set is that it covers only ten developed OECD countries plus a "rest of world" group and only two factors of production, labor and capital. However, the availability of comparable production figures from the OECD tables allowed them to test production specifications of their models as well as the trade specifications. The production test involves determining how closely a model's measured factor content of *production* corresponds to the predicted factor content of *production* and involves regressing the measured factor content of production on the predicted factor content of production. A slope coefficient of unity indicates a perfect fit between the two measures. In the case of the standard HOV model, this involves comparing a country's measured factor content of production, namely its net output premultiplied by the matrix of total factor inputs of one of the countries in the sample (typically that of the United States), with the country's factor content estimated from independent information on its factor supplies. The trade test consists of determining the closeness of the match between the measured factor content of *trade* and the predicted factor content of *trade*. One means of implementing this trade test is to compare the proportion of sign matches between the actual measured factor content of trade and the value predicted by regression analysis.

The production specification of the model performs poorly when either the US technology matrix or the average technology matrix of all the countries in the sample is used. With US technology, the slope from the regression of the measured factor content of production on the predicted factor content of production is 0.24, and it only rises to 0.33 when an average technology matrix is utilized.

Consistent with the results of tests by BLS, Trefler, and earlier authors, Davis and Weinstein found that the standard HOV trade model performs very badly in terms of the sign test with their new data set. For example, the proportion of sign matches between measured trade (using the US technology matrix) and predicted trade is only 0.32. Using the average technology of the ten OECD countries raises this proportion to 0.45. Davis and Weinstein also found that the unmodified HOV model performs poorly in terms of goodness of fit between actual and predicted factor-content trade.

Introducing best-fit, Hicks-neutral technology differences across countries does not raise the proportion of sign matches between the factor content of measured and predicted trade beyond what would be expected from the toss of a coin. The proportion of sign matches increases only from 0.45 to 0.50 in their data set. The introduction of these technological differences among countries does greatly improve the fit between the measured and predicted factor content of *production*, however. The slope coefficient increases to 0.89, but there continue to be substantial prediction errors for particular countries or country groups, such as the United Kingdom, Canada, and the rest of the world (ROW). Moreover, like BLS (1987) and Trefler (1995), the authors fail to present a theoretical model explaining how these technology parameters are determined and why they should vary across countries.

Significant improvement in their trade specification occurred only when Davis and Weinstein went beyond introducing Hicks-neutral technology differences across countries and permitted nonneutral differences in input technique. In estimating the different input matrices among countries, they utilized a hypothesis for which Dollar et al. (1988) found strong empirical support, namely that industry input usage is correlated with country factor abundance. The higher a country's capital/labor endowment ratio, for example, the more capital per worker it uses in the goods on which it specializes. Dollar et al. (1988) attribute this result to a breakdown of factor price equalization among countries: that is, countries produce in separate cones of diversification. Utilizing this relationship, Davis and Weinstein modified their common input matrix by introducing not only Hicks-neutral differences in technology across countries (this results in input coefficients differing among countries due to different country-specific productivity parameters) but by also taking into account country differences in capital/labor endowment ratios (this leads to country-specific uniform relative changes in the input coefficients of a particular factor, e.g., capital, across all traded and nontraded goods).[14] The resulting estimates of the different technology matrices across countries are then used to construct the factor content of trade in the respective countries by using the input coefficients of the countries actually producing the goods. These are then compared to the predicted factor content of trade for the countries.[15]

Permitting relative factor prices and thus relative factor inputs to differ among countries by taking into account differences in capital/labor endowment ratios across countries raises the proportion of sign matches between measured and predicted trade from the 0.50 obtained by introducing

Hicks-neutral technological differences across countries to 0.86, or a level much better than what would be expected by chance.[16] However, the fit between measured and predicted production improves only modestly from the high level already attained by introducing neutral differences in technologies. Thus modifying the assumption of factor price equalization by introducing neutral technology differences across countries and then adding Helpman's relationship, where countries are in different cones of factor proportions and specialize on different sets of traded goods, seems to be key to improving the performance of the trade specification and thereby provides empirical support for Ohlin's hypothesis that differences in relative factor supplies among countries are an important factor accounting for the differences in the pattern of trade among these countries.[17]

As Davis and Weinstein (2001a, p. 1444) recognized, a possible source of error in their calculations is the assumption that intermediate goods used in the production of exports are all of national origin. Consequently their measure of the factor content of exports embodying imported intermediates incorrectly treat these intermediates as being produced with domestic rather than foreign factors of production. Their methodology also fails to account properly for domestic factors embodied as intermediates in imported goods. They "suspect these errors are not large, but they are worthy of careful examination" (p. 1444).

Reimer (2006) developed a methodological framework that correctly measures the factor content of trade in a non–factor price equalization model that includes traded intermediates. He then estimated the significance of his methodology empirically by comparing predictions of the factor content of trade using the traditional procedure for handling intermediates followed by Davis and Weinstein to comparable predictions using his own corrected procedure for measuring the factor content of intermediates.[18] He concludes: "While this article's results do not strongly reject their supposition [that of Davis and Weinstein], the bias is ever present and tends to overstate the performance of refined models of factor service trade.... Treating all intermediates as non-traded biases measured use of locally abundant factors upward, and measured use of inabundant factors downward. This tends to overstate the measured factor content of production, demand, and trade" (Reimer 2006, p. 405).[19] Another manifestation of this point is that the capital/labor endowment ratios of the US and the ROW tend to converge. In terms of direct capital/labor ratios, the US ratio is 83.6 percent higher than that of the ROW, whereas it is only 53.9 percent greater than the comparable ROW ratio after trade in intermediate is properly taken into account.

The modifications of Davis and Weinstein in dealing with the demand side of the HOV model also differ considerably from those introduced by other testers of this model. They used the gravity equation, which emphasizes the role of distance, to model bilateral trade volumes between countries. After estimating bilateral import demand from the gravity equation, they set demand for domestically produced goods equal to the difference between the country's total demand in a particular sector and total imports predicted from the gravity equation. The appropriate factor usage matrices for each trading partner are used to generate predicted bilateral absorption of tradables in factor content terms. Adding this gravity-based demand specification to the technology modification on the production side raises the sign match in the trade specification from 0.86 to 0.91. As the authors note, this method of estimating demand "represents a substantial step away from the conventional HOV framework" (Davis and Weinstein 2001a, p. 1436). The question arises, for example, of just how satisfactory the gravity model is in measuring trade costs. Fortunately, recent improvements in our understanding of the gravity models (e.g., Anderson and van Wincoop 2003) and of home bias in consumption (e.g., Hillberry and Hummels 2003) provide new opportunities for improving the usefulness of the Davis and Weinstein (2001a) approach.

In (2001c) Davis and Weinstein explored still another major modification of the standard HOV model involving the exchange of factor services involved in intra-industry trade. This is done within the framework of their multi-cone, non–factor price equalization model in which the factor contents of a country's exports are measured using its own input coefficients and the factor contents of its imports are measured using the input coefficients of the producing countries. However, instead of measuring trade on just a net basis, as in the HOV model, the net exchange of factors resulting from matched imports and exports is also taken into account. The authors found that even among countries in the North, that is, OECD countries, trade in factor services is large and systematically related to factor endowments. The proportion of correct sign matches for trade between more and less abundant countries is 0.85 for capital and 0.9 for labor (see their table 3).

4.5 Further Contributions

Although the research of BLS, Trefler, and Davis and Weinstein on the HOV model stands out because of their efforts to modify this model in a systematic manner and to assemble detailed multi-country data sets in doing so, other researchers have made important contributions toward evaluating and modifying this model. This section reviews some of these contributions.

4.5.1 Staiger's Test

The paper by BLS (1987) is the best-known study documenting the poor empirical performance of the HOV model in a multi-country, multi-factor framework, but at about the same time this paper was published, Staiger (1988) also showed that the HOV model does not hold empirically, using a quite different approach. As he pointed out, while the focus of the theory is on the contribution of factor endowment differences to understanding patterns of trade, its strong prediction that the factor content of trade is a linear function of national and world endowments requires that the effect of additional variables is essentially random. At the theoretical level this independence is achieved by such assumptions of the model as the existence of identical, homothetic tastes and identical, constant returns-to-scale technology. Staiger (1988) applied a specification test developed by Hausman and Taylor (1981) to the trade of 29 countries for 22 tradable sectors over two time periods to determine if the effect of excluded variables is in fact random. He found clear statistical evidence that "the linear contribution of factor endowments is not independent of other country- and factor-specific effects that combine to determine the pattern of international trade" (Staiger 1988, p. 139).[20]

4.5.2 Country-Pair Tests

As pointed out in section 2.3, Staiger, Deardorff, and Stern (1987) derived a country-pair test from the basic HOV equation that eliminates the need to have data on world endowments of productive factors. Denoting the two countries as 1 and 2 and the productive factor of interest as K (capital), their equation can be expressed as

$$[F_K^1 - \alpha F_K^2] = [K^1 - \alpha K^2], \tag{2.16}$$

where F_K^1 and F_K^2 are the net exports of capital from countries 1 and 2 to the world, respectively, K^1 and K^2 are the endowments of capital in countries 1 and 2, respectively, and α is the ratio of country 1's share of world consumption (s^1) to country 2's share of world consumption (s^2), namely $\alpha = s^1/s^2$. As explained in chapter 2, this expression states that if $\alpha = 1$, namely $s^1 = s^2$, and the exports of the services of capital to the world by country 1 are greater than those of country 2 to the world, the endowment of capital in country 1 will be greater than the endowment of capital in country 2. In the case where expenditure shares in the two countries differ, α simply controls for the difference in country size.

These authors test this relationship for the United States and Japan in 1976 for ten separate productive factors, namely professional, technical, and administrative employees; sales and clerical workers; crafts workers; operatives; laborers, except farm; farm workers; scientists and engineers; service workers; capital; and arable land by comparing the signs of the left- and right-hand sides of equation (2.16). The signs are the same for eight of the ten factors, an outcome that would be considered as providing good support for this bilateral form of the Heckscher-Ohlin proposition when compared to the sign results of the multi-country studies reviewed earlier in the chapter.[21]

The main objective of Staiger et al. (1987) is to examine differences between the predicted factor content of Japanese and US trade under the HOV model and the actual observed factor content of trade, with the aim of determining the role of protectionism in accounting for these differences. They undertake this task by comparing the left- and right-hand sides of equation (2.16) by using, first, the actual net exports to the world of the two countries and, then, estimates of what this trade would be under free trade conditions in the world based on calculations from their Michigan Model of World Production and Trade (a computable-general-equilibrium model).

The authors found that simulating free trade conditions did not change any of the sign matches they obtained using actual 1976 trade. The magnitude of the differences between the two sides of the equation decreased somewhat for eight of the ten factors, but they conclude "that protection is a relatively minor element in accounting for the HO theory's empirical shortcomings and ultimately leaves unexplained the largest part of the difference between the observed trading positions of the United States and Japan and what is theoretically expected" (p. 463).

Brecher and Choudhri (1988) tested a stronger version of the country-pair relationship that involves a comparison of the actual quantities of the left- and right-hand sides of equations such as (2.16). As pointed out in section 2.3, their variant states that the amount of a particular factor embodied in a dollar of domestic expenditures of two countries must be the same if the HOV model holds for these two countries. Comparing per dollar expenditures between the United States and Canada for a breakdown of fourteen factors of production in years 1963, 1971, and 1979, the authors found that the percentage deviations for expenditures on aggregate natural resources, capital, and labor "do not appear to be large" (p. 11). However, when they broke natural resources and labor into various subgroups, their results indicated that per dollar amounts differ significantly for these subgroups, "thereby casting doubt on the two-country version of the HOV model" (p. 14).

Others who applied the sign match test of Staiger, Deardorff, and Stern (1987), using several pairs of countries, include Hakura (1999, 2001, 2002) and Debaere (2003). Hakura (2001, 2002) compared the left- and right-hand sides of equation (2.16) by employing, first, the German factor requirements in making all country-pair calculations and, then, the actual factor requirements of each country. She describes the first approach as implementing the "strict HOV model" and the second approach as presenting her "modified HOV model." She utilized 1970 and 1980 data on four of the original six members of the European Community, namely Belgium, France, Germany, and the Netherlands, which have comparably classified input–output tables. Country-pair sign comparisons are made for land, capital, manual workers, professional and administrative workers, sales and technical workers, and clerical staff.

Hakura found that the percentage of country-pair matches correctly indicating which of the two countries was more abundant from a world trade viewpoint in a factor to be much higher under her modified HOV model than her strict HOV model. Under the strict HOV model, the two sides of equation (2.16) matched in sign in 1970 in only 58 percent of the cases analyzed compared to 94 percent under the modified model. In 1980 the percentages were 47 and 86 percent, respectively.

She concluded from these results that international differences in production techniques contribute significantly to explaining differences in factor trade among countries. These differences in production techniques could be due to different technologies all together among countries or to the existences of identical technologies but countries operating at different points on the same production function. As she notes, the latter situation could arise because of differences in relative factor prices brought about by the existence of trade barriers among the countries or because countries are operating on different courses of diversification.

Plots of the predicted factor contents of trade against the actual observed factor contents of trade indicate a much better match (in the sense of the plots lying closer to the diagonal or 45-degree line) for the 1980 data than that for 1970. Hakura interpreted this result as evidence that trade barriers played a role in shaping the factor content of trade in the earlier year because EU trade was more restricted in 1970 than in 1980.[22] However, because the modified HOV model performed much better than the strict model in both 1980 and 1970, she concluded that differences in production functions were the more important factor.

Debaere (2003) extended the Staiger, Deardorff, and Stern (1987) analysis beyond a comparison of the signs of the differences for two countries (adjusted to take into account their relative sizes in expenditure terms) between their trade in a particular factor with the world and their endowments of this factor. He compared the double differences in signs for two countries between their consumption-shares-adjusted trade in *two* factors and their consumption-shares-adjusted endowments of the *two* factors. First, he divided the basic HOV equation for any country i and any factor k, $F_k^i = V_k^i - s^i V_k^w$ (see equation 2.7), by the country's consumption share of world consumption, s^i, and then defined the consumption-share-adjusted trade content of any factor k for country i, F_k^i/s^i, as F_k^{*i}, and the consumption-share-adjusted endowment of any factor k in country i, V_k^i/s^i, as V_k^{*i}. The basic HOV equation can then be expressed as

$$F_k^{*i} = V_k^{*i} - V_k^w. \tag{4.1}$$

Let there be two countries, 1 and 2, and two particular factors, capital (K) and labor (L). Following our previous notational procedure (for simplicity), write the HOV equations for capital for the two countries as

$$F_K^{*1} = K^{*1} - K^{*W}, \tag{4.2a}$$

$$F_K^{*2} = K^{*2} - K^{*W}. \tag{4.2b}$$

Also express the HOV equations and for labor for the two countries as

$$F_L^{*1} = L^{*1} - L^{*W}, \tag{4.3a}$$

$$F_L^{*2} = L^{*2} - L^{*W}. \tag{4.3b}$$

Debaere took the difference between the consumption-share-adjusted trade content of capital for countries 1 and 2 (the first terms in equations 4.2a and 4.2b) divided by the consumption-share-adjusted sum of the endowments of capital for countries 1 and 2 (the first terms on the right-hand sides of 4.2a and 4.2b) and subtracted from this figure the differences between the consumption-share-adjusted trade content of labor for countries 1 and 2 (the first terms in equations 4.3a and 4.3b) divided by the sum of the consumption-share-adjusted endowments of the two countries (the first terms on the right-hand sides of 4.3a and 4.3b). These adjustments yield the left-hand side of Debaere's basic equation:

$$\frac{F_K^{*1} - F_K^{*2}}{K^{*1} + K^{*2}} - \frac{F_L^{*1} - F_L^{*2}}{L^{*1} + L^{*2}} = \frac{K^{*1} - K^{*2}}{K^{*1} + K^{*2}} - \frac{L^{*1} - L^{*2}}{L^{*1} + L^{*2}}. \tag{4.4}$$

The right-hand side of (4.4) is the *difference* between the consumption-shares-adjusted endowments of capital between the two countries divided by the *sum* of the consumption-shares-adjusted endowments of the two countries minus the *difference* between the consumption-shares adjusted endowments of labor of the two countries divided by the *sum* of the consumption-adjusted endowments of labor of the two countries. Thus Debaere tested whether the double difference in the normalized factor contents of trade for the two countries on the left-hand side of the equality has the same sign as the double difference of their normalized endowments on the right-hand side.

In testing this bilateral form of the Heckscher-Ohlin proposition, Debaere utilized the 1983 data set of Trefler (1995), which covered 33 countries and four of the nine factors for which Trefler collected data, namely, capital, land, skilled and unskilled labor. These four factors generate six ratios: skilled/unskilled labor, skilled labor/land, skilled labor/capital, unskilled labor/land, unskilled labor/capital, and capital/land. He also added a capital/total labor ratio. For each ratio, he generated all possible 528 country pairs for the 33 countries.

The average unweighted proportion of sign matches for all the seven pairs is 71 percent with the lowest percentage (for skilled labor/capital) being 60 percent and the highest (capital/land) 77.5 percent. Thus Debaere's average ratio of 71 percent is considerably higher than Trefler's unweighted figure of 50 percent that Trefler obtained by comparing, one factor at a time, the level of a country's endowment with the level for the world in order to predict a country's factor content of trade.

As Debaere noted, his bilateral test need not produce the same overall results as Trefler's traditional multilateral unweighted sign test, but "one may wonder why the outcome is so different." (Debaere 2003, p. 606). He reasoned that the greater variations in factor endowment ratios that occur when a country's endowments are compared to those in another country rather than to the world as a whole should provide a more powerful test of the Heckscher-Ohlin relationship and thus may lead to the better results. This relationship is supported by his finding that a comparison of North–South pairs of countries raised the proportion of sign matches to 83.5 percent. Interestingly Debaere also found that introducing Hicks-neutral productivity differences among countries produced only minor sign test results. As he pointed out, his double-differences technique of carrying out the sign tests algebraically makes his results much less sensitive to neutral productivity differences.

One other noteworthy result from Debaere's analysis deserve to be stressed. It is that the percentage of sign matches increases appreciably when he compares only developed–developing country pairs. For example, the percentage of sign matches for the capital/labor ratio rises from 77 percent to 88.5 percent.

In summary, country-pair tests of the HO proposition by various authors have thus far produced results that vary widely depending on such factors as the nature of the countries analyzed, the extent of detail in the breakdown of productive factors, and the particular form of the pairwise test utilized. It is important to determine more precisely just why these differences exists.

4.5.3 *Country and Industry Technology Differences, Intra-industry Trade, and Increasing Returns*

Research by James Harrigan (1995, 1997, 2003) focuses on estimating the importance across countries of relative technology levels and relative factor supplies in determining product specialization. With data on ten OECD countries from 1970 to 1990 for two-digit ISIC manufacturing industries and six factors of production, Harrigan (1997) used a translog function to estimate industry value-added shares of countries' GDP as a function of Hick's-neutral, industry-specific technology differences across countries and time and of national factor endowments. By using this functional form, technology differences can be modeled as differences across countries that are still the same across sectors within any country (as is the case in Trefler 1995 and Davis-Weinstein 2001a), or as simultaneous differences across countries and sectors within a country.[23]

Harrigan's main results is that both technology and factor supplies are important in explaining patterns of specialization among OECD countries. However, he argued (see Harrigan 2003, p. 95) that the modeling of technological differences by Trefler (1995) and Davis and Weinstein (2002a) "may or may not be appropriate for studies of the factor content of trade, but they are too restrictive for studying comparative advantage, as they rule out all but very special types of cross-country technology differences."

As explained in section 2.4, in the "new" trade theory with differentiated products, intra-industry trade is motivated by consumer demand for a variety of similar but not identical products of an industry. In the Krugman (1979) version of this model, varieties of an industry product do not differ in their factor use, so there is no net exchange of embodied factors involved in this trade. Two studies challenging this proposition are Davis and Weinstein (2001c) and Schott (2003b).

Davis and Weinstein (2001c) analyzed the factor content of intra-industry trade for 34 sectors (equivalent to ISIC three- or four-digit data) among 10 OECD countries using the actual technology matrices of the countries.[24] Under the conventional procedure for measuring the factor content of trade, where the technology matrix of one country (usually the United States) is used to measure the factor content of every country's trade, there is no net exchange between the country and the rest of the world in any factor to the extent that a country's exports and imports of a particular product are equal in value. However, if different technology matrices are used to measure each country's factor content of trade, a net exchange of a factor is obviously possible under these circumstances. In undertaking this exercise for matched trade, the authors found that intra-industry trade is economically large and systematically related to the relative factor endowments of the countries. The median ratio of intra-industry trade to total factor trade in capital and labor is 34 percent in their country sample.

Schott (2003b) utilized detailed US import data on manufactures to investigate differences in techniques used in producing products defined at the most detailed level available, namely the ten-digit level under the harmonized system.[25] He found that by 1994 the share of these products imported from at least one low-wage country and one high-wage country is 68 percent. Moreover there is a significant positive relationship between unit-values of products and per capita GDP in the exporting countries and between unit-values and both exporting countries' capital per worker and skill level per worker. These relationships are consistent with the existence of multiple cones of product varieties in which countries relatively abundant in skilled labor and capital specialize in vertically distinct varieties that intensively use these factors. In contrast, countries abundant in unskilled labor and scarce in capital specialize in product varieties that intensively utilize this endowment structure.

There are comparatively few recent studies by empirical trade economists that explore in detail the importance of increasing returns in influencing the pattern of a country's production and trade, although Ohlin (1933) strongly emphasized the importance of this condition. Among those authors who have undertaken this difficult task are Antweiler and Trefler (2002). They investigate the relationship between industry output and trade revealed industry costs. They constructed a database covering 34 goods-producing industries for 71 countries over the period 1972 to 1992. For about one-third of all industries they found scale elasticities to range to range from 1.10 to 1.20, that is, a 1 percent increase in output is associated with a 0.10 to 0.20 fall in average costs. Another third shows constant returns to scale, while the data for the last third are not sufficiently informative to make inferences about scale. One difficulty in drawing conclusions from their results is that their scale estimates are unable to distinguish among plant-level scale economies, industry-level externalities, and scale-biased technical change. However, in comparing the unmodified HOV model against their model, which includes both neutral differences in technology across countries and their scale parameters, the authors found a significant improvement of the latter model over the former in accounting for missing trade. But the proportion of correctly predicted signs of measured trade remains at two-thirds under both approaches.

Davis and Weinstein (2003) also contribute to the increasing returns literature in an imaginative manner by testing a model that measures the concept of the "home market effect" developed in the new economic geography literature pioneered by Krugman (1980). In a trade model with increasing returns and trade costs, increases in the demand for a good enable the country to expand production of the good and realize the cost reductions associated with scale economies. Consequently a relatively high demand for a good tends to enable the country to export the good, whereas in a decreasing-returns model the country would tend to import the good at relatively high levels of demand. In measuring what they describe as "idiosyncratic derived demand," or the extent to which a country's relative demand (domestic plus foreign) for a good within an industry differs from that in the rest of the world, the authors utilized the gravity model to estimate the degree to which distance of a country from other countries causes foreign demand for a product to decline.[26]

They then compared their resulting measures of idiosyncratic derived demand for a good to the difference between a country's relative production of the good within the corresponding industry and the rest of the world's relative production of the good within the corresponding industry. These regressions indicate how production distortions move with demand distortions. A coefficient greater than unity on the idiosyncratic derived demand variable for a good is an indication of increasing returns in the production of the good, since trade costs in a constant returns to scale model would yield positive coefficients that would be less than unity. In a frictionless world of comparative advantage there would be no correlations between the two variables. They found that one-half of the 50 four-digit sectors in their data set have coefficients larger than unity, with 11 of these being significantly greater than unity. They conclude that both comparative advantage and increasing returns are important in affecting the structure of OECD manufacturing production.

4.5.4 The Helpman Test

As explained in chapter 2, Helpman (1984a) rigorously established a relationship that holds under free trade conditions between two countries with access to identical, constant returns-to-scale technology but whose factor prices are not equalized and whose preferences may or may not be identical. This relationship can be expressed in equation terms as

$$(w^j - w^i)(F^{ij} - F^{ji}) \geq 0, \tag{2.25}$$

where w^j and w^i are the vectors of factor prices in the two trading countries, F^{ij} is the gross import vector of factor content by country j from country i measured with the technology matrix employed in the exporting country i, and similarly F^{ji} is the gross import vector of factor content by country i from country j measured with the technology matrix employed in the exporting country j.

Choi and Krishna (2004) implement equation (2.25) empirically by collecting input and use data on factors and domestic intermediates, as well as bilateral trade information for eight countries (Denmark, France, Germany, the Netherlands, the United Kingdom, the United States, Canada, and Korea) for seventeen industrial sectors. In addition they assembled factor price data for each country on capital, production workers, and nonproduction workers. Alternatively, factor price data for each country were also collected on capital, production workers, and three groups of nonproduction workers. All data pertain to 1980 and are expressed in 1980 dollars.

In undertaking their calculation, the authors argued that it is first necessary to take into account a point made by Staiger (1986) concerning intermediate inputs that are freely traded. Staiger showed with a simple numerical example where there is an imported intermediate input that in Helpman's model with international differences in equilibrium factor prices but identical production functions only direct (rather than direct plus indirect) factor content measurements should be used in empirically calculating equation (2.25).[27] Consequently the input–output output matrices used by Choi and Krishna (2004) in their test include only domestically produced intermediates.

In order to provide notions of how significant departures from sign matches are, Choi and Krishna (2004) rewrote equation (2.25) as

$$\frac{w^j F^{ji} + w^i F^{ij}}{w^i F^{ji} + w^j F^{ij}} \geq 1, \tag{4.5}$$

where the numerator of this expression is the hypothetical cost of the factor content of imports from another country at the factor prices of the importing country and the denominator is the actual cost of the factor content of imports from another country at the factor prices of the exporting country. If the Heckscher-Ohlin proposition holds bilaterally, the ratio of these two sums is greater than unity.

The authors found strong empirical support for the bilateral Heckscher-Ohlin proposition. Under alternative measures of capital and groupings of workers, from 21 to 24 of the 28 bilateral trade pairs (i.e., 75 and 86 percent respectively) yield ratios for the left-hand side of (4.5) that equal or exceed unity. Moreover no more than three country pairs are below 0.99 in these various combinations.[28] Unfortunately, the study covers only a relatively small number of developing countries because comparable input–output tables are lacking for developing countries.

4.6 Conclusions

The period following the first large-scale multi-country, multi-factor study by BLS in 1987 significantly increased our knowledge about the economic forces shaping the factor content of trade among counties. An early important finding from multi-country, multi-factor studies was extensive evidence supporting the results of earlier studies that the factor content of trade could not be explained solely by differences in relative factor endowments. BLS found, for example, that the sign of actual net exports of factors matched the net export sign predicted by the HOV equation only in about 50 percent of the time, or not much better than would be expected by chance. The Trefler (1995) and Davis-Weinstein (2001a) studies obtained the same result.

Determining just what economic forces shape trading patterns and, in particular, the importance of relative factor endowments has proved considerably more difficult, however. BLS (1987) attempted to improve on the fit between measured and predicted net exports of factors by modifying the model to permit Hicks-neutral differences in technology across countries, but they still reached the conclusion that the modified Heckscher-Ohlin model "does poorly" (BLS 1987, p. 805). Fortunately, Trefler's (1995) recalculations of these calculations revealed a statistical error by BLS that, when corrected, resulted in a greatly improved fit between measured and predicted net factor trade. However, this modification does not improve the sign test for the Heckscher-Ohlin proposition. The actual sign performance is still only about as good as a coin-toss prediction. It is only with the further model modifications introduced by Davis and Weinstein (2001a), using a much richer 1995 data set than available to previous investigators, that the Heckscher-Ohlin proposition receives strong empirical support. These adjustments include permitting nonuniform differences in technology and a breakdown of factor price equalization that leaves countries in different cones of diversification. More recent studies by such authors as Debaere (2003), Schott (2003a,b), and Choi and Krishna (2004) reconfirmed the Davis and Weinstein findings of strong empirical support for the proposition that relative factor endowments are important in shaping trading patterns. However, the final models are very different from the standard Heckscher-Ohlin-Vanek framework.

5

Testing for Stolper-Samuelson, Rybczynski, and Factor Price Equalization Effects

As stated in chapter 1, the empirical review in this monograph focuses mainly on how well the factor-content version of the HO proposition conforms to countries' actual data on relative factor supplies, commodity patterns of trade, and factor-input requirements for goods, and services. However, as the analytical review of HO trade models in chapter 2 indicates, predictions about important economic relationships other than the factor-content of trade have also been made from the basic insights of Heckscher and Ohlin. This chapter reviews selected empirical investigations into three sets of such predictions: the relationship between relative changes in product prices and relative changes in factor prices (Stolper-Samuelson effects), the relationship between changes in relative factor supplies and changes in the composition of output (Rybczynski effects), and the relationship between trade and the equalization of factor prices (factor price equalization effects). The investigations have generally not been as comprehensive or rigorous as those on the Heckscher-Ohlin proposition in its factor content form, but they nevertheless yield many useful insights about the general equilibrium effects of international trade.

5.1 Stolper-Samuelson Effects

5.1.1 *General Methodological Approaches*

As noted in the discussion of the Stolper-Samuelson theorem in chapter 2, Stolper and Samuelson (1941) were well
aware that a relative increase in the domestic price of one
of the two goods in a standard two-good, two-factor HO
model results in an increase in the return to one of the factors and a decrease in the return to the other factor no matter what the reason for the change in relative product prices.
They chose, however, to explain their theorem by assuming
that the reason for the change in relative product prices
within a country is its shift from a position of autarky to
one of free trade. Empirical investigations of the relationship
between changes in product prices and changes in factor
prices have largely continued to follow this framework of
examining the effects of international trade on factor prices.

Three empirical approaches followed by researchers in
searching for Stolper-Samuelson effects are examined here.
(The empirical findings from utilizing these approaches
are discussed in the next section.) The first (and earliest)
method utilizes a political economy framework to examine
the lobbying and voting behavior of labor and capital owners *across* industries versus *within* industries in response to
proposed trade-liberalizing or protectionist legislation.[1] A
finding that the relatively scarce factor (labor, in the case of
the United States) favors protectionist policies no matter
whether it is employed in an import-competing or export-
oriented industry, whereas owners of capital (the abundant
factor) support trade-liberalizing legislation regardless of
its industry of employment would be consistent with the
Stolper-Samuelson proposition. In contrast, a finding that

the trade-policy views of both factors tend to be the same in any industry would be consistent with the specific-factors model rather than the HO model on which the Stolper-Samuelson proposition is based.

A second methodology is based on the "correlation" version of the Stolper-Samuelson theorem and regresses relative changes in industry product prices over a particular period on various measures of factor use by industry. This technique has been used to investigate the role of relative price pressures from foreign sources in accounting for the increase in the wages of skilled workers relative to unskilled workers, namely an increase in wage inequality, in countries that are relatively abundant in their endowment of skilled labor and relatively scarce in their supply of unskilled labor. One example of this approach models the United States as a small price-taking economy facing prices determined exogenously abroad and regresses changes in US manufacturing prices across industries over a particular time period on the ratio of the use of skilled to unskilled labor across the industries at the outset of the period. The finding of a negative coefficient on the ratio of industry employment of skilled to unskilled workers, namely the more skill-intensive an industry, the smaller the increase in the industry's relative price, would *not* be consistent with the hypothesis that Stolper-Samuelson price effects originating abroad were the dominant factor contributing to the rise in the wages of skilled workers relative to unskilled workers. In contrast, a statistically significant positive coefficient would be consistent with this hypothesis. But, if the United States is in fact not a small price-taking economy, this latter result could also be consistent with changes in domestic conditions, such as unskilled labor-saving technical progress that, in addition to increasing the wages of skilled relative to unskilled labor directly, reduces the prices of unskilled labor-intensive products compared with skilled labor-intensive goods and partly offsets an increase in the relative wages of skilled labor.

Another example of this second methodology utilizes the zero-profit conditions that exist in the standard HO model with perfect competition and perfect mobility of factors domestically. This condition can be written as

$$\hat{p}_i = \sum_{k=1}^{M} \theta_{ki} \hat{w}_k, \tag{5.1}$$

where $\hat{p}_i$ is the proportional change in the price of any of the N products, $\hat{w}_k$ is the proportional change in the return to any of the M factors, and θ_{ki} is the distributive share of the kth factor in the production of the ith good (where $\sum_{k=1}^{M} \theta_{ki} = 1$).[2] In words, for small changes in factor prices, the relative change in the price of any good is equal to the weighted sum of the relative changes in the prices of the factors of production, where the weights are the shares of the respective factors used in producing a unit value of the good.

For the traditional two-good, two-factor HOS model, equation (5.1) implies that an increase in the relative price of one of the goods increases the real wage of the factor used intensively in producing that good and lowers the real wage of the other factor. This is the "essential" version of the Stolper-Samuelson theorem. As pointed out in chapter 2, with more than two goods and two factors, only on average will factors used intensively in rising-price sectors themselves rise in price, while factors used intensively in falling-price sectors will fall in price. This relationship says nothing about any particular product or factor price, which may rise or fall. However, equation (5.1) can be used to estimate proportional changes in factor prices in a given period by regressing observed proportionate changes in product prices across industries on industry factor shares in the base period. The estimated coefficients on the factor share are—to use Leamer (1998, p. 179) term—the "mandated" changes in factor prices associated with the observed changes in product prices in order to keep the zero-profit condition operative. The regression equation is

$$\hat{p}_i = \sum_{k=1}^{M} \theta_{ki}\hat{w}_k + e_j, \tag{5.2}$$

where e_j is a well-behaved error term, and the coefficients of the distributive shares for the various factors are the estimated proportionate changes in returns for these factors. Thus, if it is assumed that the country is "small" and faces fixed prices of commodities internationally, a finding of a statistically significant increase in the coefficient of the distributive share of skilled labor relative to the coefficient on the distributive share of unskilled labor would be consistent with the view that increased foreign competition was the main cause of the increased wage inequality.

In a third approach, best-known to trade economists from the work of Kohli (1990, 1991), Harrigan (1997), and Harrigan and Balaban (1999), researchers do not attempt to isolate the effect of changes in international trade on wages, but rather to estimate separately the effects of changes in product prices, technology and endowments on changes in relative wages. Harrigan and Balaban begin by expressing a country's gross domestic product (G) as a function of technology levels, supplies of capital, and supplies of different types of factors. Specifically, national revenue is expressed as

$$G = r(\delta p, V, t), \tag{5.3}$$

where δ is a scalar parameter representing Hicks-neutral technological progress in an industry relative to a base period, p denotes the prices of the N final products, V denotes the supplies of the M factors, and t denotes technical change other than Hicks-neutral that is indexed by time.

The authors follow Kohli (1991) in assuming that a country's GDP function can be well approximated by a translog function written as

$$\ln G = a_{00} + \sum_{i=1}^{N} a_{0i} \ln \delta_{it} p_{it} + \frac{1}{2} \sum_{i=1}^{N} \sum_{j=1}^{N} a_{ij} \ln \delta_{it} p_{it} \cdot \ln \delta_{jt} p_{jt}$$

$$+ \sum_{k=1}^{M} b_{0k} \ln V_{kt} + \frac{1}{2} \sum_{k=1}^{M} \sum_{l=1}^{M} b_{kl} \ln V_{kt} \cdot \ln V_{lt}$$

$$+ \sum_{i=1}^{N} \sum_{k=1}^{M} c_{ik} \ln \delta_{it} p_{it} \cdot \ln V_{kt}$$

$$+ t \cdot \sum_{i=1}^{N} d_{0i} \ln \delta_{it} p_{it} + t \cdot \sum_{k=1}^{M} d_{1k} \ln V_{kt}$$

$$+ d_2 \cdot t + d_3 \cdot t^2, \tag{5.4}$$

where the summations over goods i and j run from 1 to N, and the summations over factors k and l run from 1 to M. Symmetry of cross effects requires $a_{ij} = a_{ji}$ and $b_{kl} = b_{lk}$ for all i, j, k, and l.[3] In addition, to ensure the GDP function is homogeneous of degree one in endowments and prices, Harrigan and Balaban impose the requirements:

$$\sum_{i=1}^{N} a_{0i} = \sum_{k=1}^{M} b_{0k} = 1,$$

$$\sum_{i=1}^{N} a_{ij} = \sum_{j=1}^{N} a_{ij} = \sum_{k=1}^{M} b_{kl} = \sum_{l=1}^{M} b_{kl} = \sum_{k=1}^{M} c_{ik} = \sum_{i=1}^{N} c_{ik} = \sum_{i=1}^{N} d_{0i}$$

$$= \sum_{k=1}^{M} d_{1k} = 0.$$

The attractiveness of the translog function is the interpretation that can be given to its first derivatives. For example, since $\partial \ln G / \partial \ln V_k = (\partial G / \partial V_k)(V_k/G)$ (where $\partial G / \partial V_k$ equals the factor price of endowment k), it follows that $(\partial G / \partial V_k)(V_k/G)$ is the share of GDP devoted to factor k, which will be denoted as s_{kt}. Computing the derivative of equation (5.3) with respect to V_k yields

$$s_{kt} = b_{0k} + \sum_{l=2}^{M} b_{kl} \ln\left(\frac{V_{lt}}{V_{1t}}\right) + \sum_{i=2}^{N} c_{ik} \ln\left(\frac{\delta_{it}p_{it}}{\delta_{1t}p_{1t}}\right) + d_{1k}t. \quad (5.5)$$

Similarly, the derivative of equation (5.3) with respect to product prices, namely, $\partial \ln G / \partial \ln p_i = (\partial G / \partial p_i)(p_i/G)$ is the share of industry i in GDP (where $\partial G / \partial p_i$ is the output of sector i) and will be denoted as s_{it}. This differentiation yields[4]

$$s_{it} = a_{0i} + \sum_{k=2}^{M} c_{ik} \ln\left(\frac{V_{jt}}{V_{1t}}\right) + \sum_{j=2}^{N} a_{ij} \ln\left(\frac{\delta_{jt}p_{jt}}{\delta_{1t}p_{1t}}\right) + d_{0i}t. \quad (5.6)$$

The coefficients of equations (5.5) and (5.6) can be estimated econometrically with annual data on output and factor shares, product prices, endowments, and total factor productivity (TFP) (as a measure of Hicks-neutral technological progress). The linear homogeneity conditions imposed on the revenue function imply that there are $M - 1$ independent factor-share equations and $N - 1$ independent output-share equations.

Since Stolper-Samuelson effects are defined as the effect of changes in prices on the level of a factor's return rather than on its share of GDP, the conversion to this traditional expression of the relationship can be made by writing each factor price as $\ln w_{kt} = \ln(s_{kt} G/V_{kt})$ and differentiating this with respect to $\ln p^i$. Utilizing equations (5.5) and (5.6), the Stolper-Samuelson elasticities can be expressed as

$$\frac{\partial \ln w_{kt}}{\partial \ln p_{it}} = \frac{c_{ik}}{s_{kt}} + s_{it}. \tag{5.7}$$

It is these elasticities (among others) that the authors estimate and that are discussed below.

5.1.2 Empirical Findings

The Political Economy Approach
S. Magee (1980) pioneered empirical investigations that utilize the first approach discussed in the section above; namely, testing the S-S theorem by investigating the political actions and attitudes of capitalist groups versus worker groups with regard to the effects of proposed trade legislation. He examined the pro–trade-liberalizing versus pro-protectionist nature of the testimony of 29 trade associations representing management and 23 labor unions during hear-

ings held by the House Ways and Means Committee on the Trade Act of 1974. This Act gave the president authority to reduce most tariffs by as much as 60 percent, subject to an up or down vote by the Congress on the multilateral trade agreement reached by the president. The assumption of the HOS model that productive factors are perfectly mobile across industries implies that capitalists and labor in any industry should oppose each other with regard to the issue of trade liberalization or increased protection for that industry. Magee finds, however, that in 19 of 21 industries management and labor adopted the same trade-policy position in testifying before the Committee. Moreover he finds that both capitalists and labor tend to favor freer trade if there is an export surplus in their industry and favor protectionism if there is an import surplus. Two studies by Irwin (1994, 1996) also conclude that voters are more influenced by the economic conditions of the industry in which they are employed than by their relative scarcity position among the country's factor endowments. For example, Irwin's 1994 econometric analysis of the British general election of 1906 (where protectionism versus free trade was the major electoral issue) indicates that workers employed in industries heavily dependent on exports favored free trade, while those in sectors facing increasing import competition supported a policy of increased import protection. Similarly his analysis of voting in the 1923 British general election shows that workers facing increased import competition in their industry of employment shifted in their voting pattern toward favoring increased import protection.

There are, however, a number of more recent studies of trade-policy behavior that support the implications of the Stolper-Samuelson theorem.[5] Beaulieu (2002), for example, finds that factor type (skilled labor versus unskilled labor in his study) played a statistically significant role in accounting for the views of Canadian voters on the Canada–US Free Trade Agreement. However, his analysis also indicates that industry of employment helps determine preferences on trade policy.

In investigating the determinants of a country's trade policy, Scheve and Slaughter (2001) also utilize use a direct measure of policy preferences rather than lobbying or voting behavior as the dependent variable in order to avoid endogeneity problems in the interpretation of regression results. They base their analysis on a 1993 National Election Studies random survey of the US population concerning whether the respondents "favor or oppose placing new limits on imports, or haven't you thought much about this?" Scheve and Slaughter (2001, p. 275). Like Beaulieu, these authors find that the skill level of the respondent plays a significant role in determining trade policy preferences. The higher the skill levels of respondents, the lower the probability of supporting protectionist trade legislation. Higher industry trade exposure has ambiguous effects. Interestingly, their analysis also reveals that in counties with a mix of manufacturing concentrated in comparative-disadvantage industries, home ownership is strongly correlated with support for trade barriers.

Beaulieu and C. Magee (2004) revisit S. Magee's (1980) lobbying approach in searching for Stolper-Samuelson effects by utilizing a much more comprehensive dataset than was available for the earlier study. In particular, Beaulieu and C. Magee are able to identify in a much more detailed manner the contributions of corporate and labor political action committees (PACs) by industry and by factor affiliation in their analysis of lobbying behavior related to congressional votes on the North American Free Trade

Agreement and the GATT Uruguay Round Agreements. Their regressions support the conclusions of Beaulieu (2002) and Scheve and Slaughter (2001) that the factor a group represents influences views on trade policy more than industry characteristics do. PACs representing the interests of capitalists contribute to candidates supporting trade liberalization regardless of the net export position of the industry that the PAC represents. There is, however, some evidence that contributions of labor PACs differ across industries.

The reason for the difference between their findings (as well as those of other recent researchers) and the 1980 findings of S. Magee is, Beaulier and C. Magee (2004) suggest, that lobbying groups considered the 1974 Trade Act to be a short-term measure whereas the effects of NAFTA and the Uruguay Round Agreements were regarded as having more long-term consequences.

While studies by economists of lobbying and voting behavior when legislatures are considering trade-liberalizing or protectionist actions have greatly improved our understanding of the political-economy processes by which trade policy is made, the authors recognize that they cannot be regarded as rigorous empirical tests of the Stolper-Samuelson proposition. This approach not only fails to provide independent information on the relative use of capital versus labor in the industries that the lobbying groups are representing but simply assumes the groups know the manner in which a particular piece of trade legislation will affect product prices and thus factor returns. No analysis in presented concerning the likely price effects of the proposed legislation or the actual price consequences of similar previous legislation. The possibility that other economic forces such as technological changes may explain the observed relationships are also not carefully explored.

Product-Price Studies

Lawrence and Slaughter (1993) is one of the earliest studies based on the second approach described in the previous subsection; namely, using industry price and factor-use data to analyze the effect of international trade on relative wages.[6] Assuming the United States to be a small, price-taking economy, they regress changes in three sets of manufacturing prices over the 1980s: imports, exports, and domestic production on each manufacturing industry's ratio of its direct employment of nonproduction to production workers. Their main finding for all three price series and various weighting methods is that the coefficient relating industry skill-intensity ratios to price changes is either zero or negative. They interpret this result as evidence against the hypothesis that changes in international trade accounted for the widening gap between the wages of non-production to production workers. Using methodologies unrelated to trade theory, another influential early study by Berman, Bound, and Griliches (1994) also concludes that the role of trade in shifting employment away from US manufacturing industries intensively using production workers to be quite small.

Leamer (1998) does not make the assumption that economic developments in the United States have no effect on domestic prices in his formal analysis of product-price changes. Instead, he assumes that relative changes in factor prices are influenced by two forces operating on changes in value-added product prices: changes due to domestic technological progress, t, and changes due to globalization, g. The changes in value-added prices due to these two forces are expressed as $\hat{p}_i(t) - \gamma_i \hat{p}(t)$ and $\hat{p}_i(g) - \gamma_i \hat{p}(g)$, respectively, where γ_i is the materials inputs share for any good i. Technological change is measured by total factor-productivity growth $(\widehat{\text{TFP}})$ and is assumed to affect only value-added prices. Furthermore the fraction of productivity gains passed on to consumers in the form of lower value-added prices, namely λ, is assumed to be the same in every industry and taken to be either 1 or zero in Leamer's empirical calculations. Thus the price pass-through to value-added prices from technical change is

$$\hat{p}_i(t) - \gamma_i \hat{p}(t) = -\lambda \widehat{\text{TFP}}_i. \tag{5.8}$$

The zero-profit equation can be written as

$$\hat{p}_i = \sum_{k=1}^{M} \theta_{ki} \hat{w}_k + \gamma_i \hat{p}_i - \widehat{\text{TFP}}_i, \tag{5.9}$$

where $\hat{p}_i$ is the proportional change in the price of any of the N products, θ_{ki} is the distributive cost share of the kth factor in the production of the ith good, $\hat{w}_k$ is the proportional change in the costs of any of the M factors, $\gamma_i \hat{p}_i$ is the relative change in the cost share of materials inputs, and $\widehat{\text{TFP}}_i$ is total factor productivity growth in any of the N sectors. As Leamer (1998, p. 181) notes, moving the product-price term on the right-hand side to the left yields "a Stolper-Samuelson system of equations that implicitly define a mapping of 'value-added' prices into factor prices," that is, $\hat{p}_i - \gamma_i \hat{p}_i = \sum_{k=1}^{M} \theta_{ki} \hat{w}_k - \widehat{\text{TFP}}_i$. He interprets the coefficients on the factor shares as the "mandated" changes in factor costs. Leamer concludes (p. 197) that if the mandated and actual changes in factor costs "conform adequately, we will argue that we have provided an accurate explanation of the trends in wages."

Substituting the right-hand side of equation (5.8) for $\hat{p}_i - \gamma_i \hat{p}$ and collecting terms, the effect of technological progress on factor prices can be written as

$$(1 - \lambda)\widehat{\text{TFP}}_i = \sum_{k=1}^{M} \theta_{ki}\hat{w}_k(t). \tag{5.10}$$

Since the actual change in value-added prices minus the change in value-added prices due to technical change equals the effect of changes in value-added prices due to globalization, the globalization effect on factor prices is

$$\hat{p}_i + \lambda\widehat{\text{TFP}}_i = \sum_{k=1}^{M} \theta_{ki}\hat{w}_k(g) + \gamma_i\hat{p}. \tag{5.11}$$

Adding an error term to equations (5.10) and (5.11), Leamer uses regressions to estimate separately the effect of sectoral growth in pass-through-adjusted TFP on factor prices (5.10) and the effect of changes in product-prices adjusted for TFP-induced changes in these prices on factor prices (5.11). Leamer (1998, p. 178) recognizes, however, that, if the United States is not a "small" country, he may be "putting the 'globalization' label onto something strictly internal to the United States."

Leamer presents a variety of data and statistical measures relating to trends in wage inequality over the three periods on which he focuses, namely 1961 to 1971, 1971 to 1981, and 1981 to 1991. In the first part of this paper, he takes average wages of production workers in the apparel industry as representing the wages of unskilled workers and considers changes in these wages relative to changes in the wages of production workers in other two-digit manufacturing sectors as indicating the behavior of skill premiums over the three time periods. He interprets the results as showing a somewhat downward trend in wage inequality in the 1960s, a definite increase in wage inequality in the 1970s, and no significant change in the degree of inequality in the 1980s. However, in the section formally analyzing the effects of globalization versus technical change on wage inequality where he presents wage data on production versus nonproduction workers, his findings are somewhat different. Taking the ratio of the earnings of nonproduction to production workers as indicating the behavior of the earnings of skilled versus unskilled workers, he finds the ratio to fall in both the 1960s and 1970s (but more in the 1960s) and rise in the 1980s. As he remarks (p. 185), this indication that most of the increase in income inequality came after 1980 is fairly similar to the finding of other researchers. However, he is skeptical about the usefulness of the production/nonproduction categories and continues to regard his initial findings as the best indicator of the actual behavior of the wages of skilled relative to unskilled workers over the periods covered.

Leamer's regressions based on equations (5.10) and (5.11) utilize data assembled by Bartelsman and Gray (1996) and cover 450 four-digit US manufacturing industries over the periods, 1961 to 1971, 1971 to 1981, and 1981 to 1991. Factor-cost shares are measured for the first year in each decade. Capital and labor are the primary factors but labor is also divided into various groupings, such as production and nonproduction workers and his own classification of high-wage and low-wage workers.[7]

The implications from the regressions over the three periods concerning the effects of globalization on wage inequality are mixed, depending upon the classification system used, the price pass-through assumption, and the decade being considered. For the 1960s, workers classified as high-wage workers by Leamer gained relative to low-wage workers under the 0 percent pass-through assumption but lose relative to low wage workers under the 100 percent pass-through assumption. A comparison of the earnings of production workers with nonproduction workers over the same decade also yields conflicting results depending on the pass-through assumption. This time, however, the lower skilled production workers gain in relative terms under the 0 pass-through assumption. In the 1970s, Leamer's low-wage workers gain appreciably in relative terns under both pass-through assumptions. Production workers also lose significantly relative to nonproduction workers under the 100 percent pass-through assumption. But, the reverse holds for this classification of workers under the zero percent pass-though assumption. The relative changes in the rewards of the two types of workers are generally less striking in the 1980s, and there are conflicting directional changes in this decade depending on the pass-through assumption.

Leamer (1998, p. 195) concludes from these various results that "the 1970s was the Stolper-Samuelson decade." He also concludes that price changes unrelated to changes in technology (his globalization effects) dominate technology effects in influencing relative wage inequality over the three periods. However, as Grossman (1998, p. 210) points out in his comments on the paper: "The regressions allow no avenue for factor-biased technological progress to affect product prices and thus factor prices, removing by assumption the main competing hypothesis put forward by the 'trade-can't-be-that-important' school." Grossman also stresses the limited conclusions one can draw from a study that covers only the manufacturing sector.

Baldwin and Cain (2000) also utilize the zero-profit conditions in analyzing shifts in relative US factor prices. However, they do not explicitly separate out the influence of technology on factor returns by including a measure of TFP growth in the econometric model. A major reason is because including TFP results in simultaneous equation bias since the usual measure of an industry's TFP growth contains variables that are endogenous to changes in output prices, for example, changes in factor and output quantities. Utilizing TFP growth by industry to measure the influence of technology on relative factor returns also fails to account for factor-biased technological progress. Yet it has often been asserted that this type of technical change is the main cause of increased wage inequality between skilled and unskilled workers (Bound and Johnson 1992; Katz and Murphy 1992; Berman, Bound, and Griliches 1994). Baldwin and Cain (2000) attempt to determine the dominant domestic or international force influencing the relative wages of US skilled and unskilled workers by supplementing regressions of industry price changes on factor shares with regression results for three other industry variables: changes in output, changes in import prices, and changes in the ratio of net exports to consumption. They do not make the assumption that the United States is a "small" country.

The regressions cover all industries as well as manufacturing industries by themselves using the two-digit industry classification of the input-output tables prepared by the Bureau of Economic Analysis of the US Commerce Department. Four time intervals are covered: 1968 to 1973, 1973 to 1979, 1979 to 1987, and 1987 to 1996, where the direct and indirect factor shares used for these periods are calculated from the input–output benchmark years 1967, 1972, 1977, and 1987, respectively. The input–output tables include data on output, consumption, exports and imports, while data on domestic prices, import prices, and employment are from publications of the Bureau of Labor Statistics of the US Labor Department. Wages by educational groups are based on surveys conducted by the Census Bureau of the US Department of Commerce. Because value-added for capital and land is measured as a residual in the input–output tables, a proxy variable, the total capital used per unit of output in each industry, is used to measure the capital–land share.

The basic regression relating price changes to factor shares is

$$\hat{p}_i = \alpha + \sum_{k=1}^{M} \theta_{ki}\hat{w}_k + \hat{r}K_i + e_i, \tag{5.12}$$

where the terms are as previously defined with the addition that K_i is the total capital used in the ith industry, $\hat{r}$ is the proportional change in capital's return, α is a constant term introduced to capture trends in prices due to errors in the right-hand side variables and to omitted variables, and e_i is a well-behaved error term.

Regressions of price changes on factor shares over the 1968 to 1973 period predict a statistically significant reduction in the wage gap between more-educated (13+ years of education) workers and less-educated (1–12 years of education) workers in both all sectors and manufacturing alone. Since the actual wage ratio of more-educated to less-educated workers for all sectors fell from 1.51 to 1.45 between 1967 and 1972, these results are consistent with the "essential" version of the Stolper-Samuelson that does not focus just on foreign-induced price changes. Over the period 1973 to 1979 when the actual wage gap continued to narrow from 1.45 to 1.38, the same predicted wage relationships holds, but it is statistically weaker. Price regressions based on equation (5.12) also indicate Stolper-Samuelson effects for the period 1979 to 1987, when the predicted widening of wages between more educated and less educated workers is confirmed by the rise in their actual wage ratio from 1.38 to 1.50. Over the final period covered, 1987 to 1996, the wage ratio of more to less educated workers rose slightly from 1.50 to 1.52. A positive but statistically insignificant increase is predicted by the price regressions covering all sectors, but a significant decline is predicted for the manufacturing sector.

The authors are mainly interested in ascertaining which of various plausible domestic or international forces are most likely to have been dominant in shaping the changes in wage ratios over the different periods. For the 1968 to 1973 and 1973 to 1979 periods, they find support for the hypothesis that the observed increase in the supply of more educated workers relative to less educated workers was the dominant economic factor lowering the wages of more educated relative to less educated workers.[8] Regressions indicating a relative shift in production toward goods intensive in the use of more educated labor and the observed increase in the average industry use ratio of more educated to less educated workers over these periods are consistent with this hypothesis. Changes in trade that act to reduce the wages of more educated workers compared with less educated workers do not seem to be a plausible explanation for the reduction in wage inequality. Regressions relating the factor shares of industries to a variable indicating changes in industries' comparative advantage—namely exports minus imports of the industries divided by the consumption of the industries' goods and services—suggest that trade forces actually operated to raise the relative demand for more educated workers over the two periods. Also no plausible technological change seems to account for the actual change in relative wages and the other variables discussed.

As the authors point out, the significant increase in wage inequality that occurred during the 1979 to 1987 and 1987 to 1996 periods obviously cannot be explained by the continued rapid growth in the supply of more educated relative to less educated workers, since this development tends to reduce the wage gap. They conclude that a combination of increased import competition in industries intensively using less educated workers and technical change that is both greater in industries intensively using highly educated labor and saving in the use of less educated labor seem to be important over this period. The increased import-competition hypothesis receives support for the 1979 to 1987 period, for example, from regressions of changes in domestic prices, import prices for manufactured goods,[9] industry output, and trade ratios on the factor-cost shares of more educated and less educated labor. It should be noted that although the signs of the coefficient differences between more educated and less educated workers are all as expected, only those for the change in domestic prices for all sectors and for changes in industry output for both all sectors and manufacturing are statistically significant. As Krugman and Lawrence (1994a) point out, if increased import competition in less educationally intensive industries is the major source of the observed change in factor prices in this period, the resulting increase in the relative wages of more educated workers should have led to substitution in production of less educated workers for more educated workers. In fact, the average industry ratio of labor with 13+ years of education used per dollar of industry output to labor with 1 to 12 years of schooling continued to increase significantly across industries. Biased technical change domestically that is saving of less educated labor will produce this relative shift in labor coefficients, but its direct effects will also raise the output of less education-intensive sectors relative to more education-intensive sectors in order to absorb the displaced labor. However, the opposite actually occurred. Thus both increased import competition and biased technical progress seem to have shaped the key economic variables during this period.

In his detailed review of product-price studies, Slaughter (2000) points out that the variable estimated in mandated wage regressions (changes in factor prices) is the regressor while the independent variable (changes in product prices) is the regressand. He concludes, consequently (see p. 151), that this approach should "be interpreted as an accounting exercise, rather than as identifying causation in the way regressions are usually presumed to."

Feenstra and Hanson (1999, 2003) modify the "mandated" factor price approach in a substantial manner. Following Feenstra's (2004, ch. 4) summary of the 1999 Feenstra and Hanson paper, specify the unit cost function for an industry as $c_i(w_i, q_i, r_i, z_i)$, where w_i, q_i, and r_i are the returns in industry i $(i = 1, \ldots, N)$ of the three productive factors in their model, namely unskilled labor (L), skilled labor (H), and physical capital (K) and z_i is a vector of structural variables that shift the production function and thus affect costs. The zero profit condition in the industries is written as

$$p_i = c_i(w_i, q_i, r_i, z_i), \qquad i = 1, \ldots, N, \tag{5.13}$$

where w_i, q_i, and r_i are as defined above and p_i is the price of the good produced in sector i.

Define total factor productivity in sector i (TFP_i) as

$$\text{TFP}_i = (\theta_{Li}\Delta\ln w_i + \theta_{Hi}\Delta\ln q_i + \theta_{Ki}\Delta\ln r_i) - \Delta\ln p_i, \tag{5.14}$$

where θ_{Li}, θ_{Hi}, and θ_{Ki} are the cost shares of the three factors, which sum to unity (i.e., $\theta_{Li} + \theta_{Hi} + \theta_{Ki} = 1$); Δ denotes the first difference; and $\ln p_i$ is the log price of the good produced in industry i. Rearranging these terms slightly yields the equation

$$\Delta \ln p_i = -\text{TFP}_i + \theta_{Li} \Delta \ln w_i + \theta_{Hi} \Delta \ln q_i + \theta_{Ki} \Delta \ln r_i,$$

$$i = 1, \ldots, N. \tag{5.15}$$

The usual next step in the product-price approach is to estimate the implied or mandated changes in factor prices β_L, β_H, β_K from the regression equation:

$$\Delta \ln p_i = -\text{TFP}_i + \theta_{Li} \beta_L + \theta_{Hi} \beta_H + \theta_{Ki} \beta_K + \varepsilon_i,$$

$$i = 1, \ldots, N, \tag{5.16}$$

where ε_i is an error term. Feenstra and Hanson reject this procedure, however, because the error term in (5.16) is likely correlated with the cost shares that are the independent variables and thus the regression estimates are biased. Instead, they deal with the bias issue by combining the error term with the TFP data to derive what they term an industry's *effective* total factor productivity, ETFP_i. This is defined as

$$\text{ETFP}_i \equiv \text{TFP}_i - \epsilon_i, \tag{5.17}$$

The error term, ϵ_i, reflects the change in the difference between factor prices paid in each manufacturing industry and the manufacturing average of each of these factor prices and can be calculated as

$$\epsilon_i = \theta_{Li}(\Delta \ln w_i - \overline{\Delta \ln w}) + \theta_{Hi}(\Delta \ln q_i - \overline{\Delta \ln q})$$

$$+ \theta_{Ki}(\Delta \ln r_i - \overline{\Delta \ln r}), \tag{5.18}$$

where $\overline{\Delta \ln w}$, $\overline{\Delta \ln q}$, and $\overline{\Delta \ln r}$ are the actual average changes in the returns of these three factors in manufacturing. Substituting this specification of the error term into the right-hand side of (5.16) and simplifying yields

$$\mathrm{ETFP}_i = (\theta_{Li}\overline{\Delta \ln w} + \theta_{Hi}\overline{\Delta \ln q} + \theta_{Ki}\overline{\Delta \ln r}) - \Delta \ln p_i. \qquad (5.19)$$

The regression in (5.16) is now written as

$$\Delta \ln p_i = -\mathrm{ETFP}_i + \theta_{Li}\beta_L + \theta_{Hi}\beta_H + \theta_{Ki}\beta_K, \qquad i = 1, \ldots, N, \qquad (5.20)$$

and does not include an error term. However, since estimates of this equation should provide a perfect fit that simply yield the actual changes in factor prices, such estimates do not provide the researcher with any new information.

To deal with this issue, the authors undertake a two-stage estimation process. In the first stage, they combine the variables $\Delta \ln p_i + \mathrm{ETFP}_i$ and regress these on the structural variables. Assuming for simplicity that there are only two structural variables, the regression they run can be expressed as

$$\Delta \ln p_i + \mathrm{ETFP}_i = \alpha_0 + \alpha_1\Delta z_{1i} + \alpha_2\Delta z_{2i}, \qquad (5.21)$$

where Δz_1 and Δz_2 are the changes in the two structural variables. In the second step, the authors then take the estimated coefficient $\hat{\alpha}_1$ times the structural variable Δz_{1i} and the estimated coefficient $\hat{\alpha}_2$ times the structural variable Δz_{2i} as dependent variables, and regress each of these on the cost shares of the three factors in their model:

$$\hat{\alpha}_1\Delta z_{1i} = \theta_{Li}\beta_{1L} + \theta_{Hi}\beta_{1H} + \theta_{Ki}\beta_{1K}, \qquad (5.22a)$$

$$\hat{\alpha}_2\Delta z_{2i} = \theta_{Li}\beta_{2L} + \theta_{Hi}\beta_{2H} + \theta_{Ki}\beta_{2K}. \qquad (5.22b)$$

The coefficients obtained on the factor shares from the second stage regressions, namely, β_{1L}, β_{1H}, β_{1K}, and β_{2L}, β_{2H}, β_{2K}, are interpreted as the portion of the total change in factor prices that are explained by that structural variable. Thus, Feenstra and Hanson take the total change in factor prices and decompose it into parts that are explained by each structural variable.

The data for estimating equations (5.21) and (5.22) are from the National Bureau of Economic Research Productivity Database (Bartelsman and Grey 1996) and cover 447 US manufacturing industries over the period 1979 to 1990. The authors use nonproduction workers as a proxy for skilled labor (H) and production workers as a proxy for unskilled labor in the regressions.[10] The wages of nonproduction workers increased by 5.44 per year during the period, while the wages of production workers increased by only 4.71 per year. Consequently the wages of skilled to nonskilled workers rose by an average of 0.73 percent per year.

Two structural variables that Feenstra and Hanson find are related in a positive and statistically significant manner to the dependent variable $\Delta\ln p_i + \text{ETFP}_i$ are foreign outsourcing (measured as the share of imported intermediates in total costs) and expenditures on computers (measured as the computer share of capital stock or the computer share of investment). Furthermore, in the second-stage regressions, they find that foreign outsourcing and capital upgrading each contribute to the widening wage gap between skilled and unskilled workers. Outsourcing accounts for about 15 percent of the increase in the relative wages of nonproduction workers and the share of capital stock (measured in *ex post* rental prices) devoted to computers for about 35 percent. While these shares are sensitive to the particular way in which outsourcing or the capital stock is measured,[11] both of these structural variables are statistically significant in the expected direction.

Estimating the Gross Domestic Product Function

As described in the preceding section on methodologies, Harrigan and Balaban (1999) specify a model that can that can be used to estimate the general equilibrium relationships between wages and technology, prices, and factor supplies. In empirically implementing the model for the US economy over the years 1963 to 1991, they divide factors and goods into four groups each. The factor breakdown is: high school dropouts, high school graduates, college graduates, and physical capital; the goods division is: nontraded goods intensive in less skilled labor, nontraded goods intensive in skilled labor, traded goods intensive in less skilled labor, and traded goods intensive in skilled labor.[12] Data on wages and employment are from the US Bureau of Census and on capital from the US Bureau of Economic Analysis. Measures of prices and technology growth were derived from a data set collected by a group of researchers headed by Dale Jorgenson of Harvard and available on Jorgenson's Web page.

Because prices are endogenous in the Harrigan-Balaban model, the authors use instruments for international and domestic prices. For international prices, they first divide all countries into four income groups depending on whether the country's per capita GDP compared to US per capita GDP in 1991 is (1) less than 25 percent, (2) 25 percent but less than 50 percent, (3) 50 percent but less than 75 percent, and (4) at least 75 percent. They next construct a measure indicating the presence of each country's labor supply in international markets, namely its labor supply multiplied by the ratio of gross trade to GDP. This labor supply variable is then summed for all countries in a particular relative income group to obtain the total effective labor supply by relative income quartile. The instruments for domestic prices include total factor productivity, factor supplies, and government expenditures as a proportion of a country's GDP.

The authors' estimations of Stolper-Samuelson elasticities, namely elasticities of nominal wages with respect to prices, indicate that overall relative price changes increased wage inequality, particularly with respect to the differential between college and high school graduates. Between 1970 and 1990 price changes brought about real wage gains to college graduates of 67 percent and a decrease in the real wages of high school graduates of 39 percent. Especially important in leading to these results was the large increase in the price of nontraded skilled services, which led to a nominal wage increase of college graduates of 134 percent and a nominal wage reduction of high school graduates of 59 percent. In contrast, price increases in nontraded unskilled intensive sectors lowered the wages of high school dropouts, while raising the wages of both high school and college graduates. Thus, price increases in the nontraded goods sector served to widen the wage gap between college-educated workers and both high school graduates and high school dropouts. Most of the Stolper-Samuelson wage elasticities for the traded-goods sector are not statistically significant. The only definite statement that can be made is that price increases in this sector increased the wages of unskilled workers with either a high school or college education.

The relatively weak results obtained by Harrigan and Balaban for the traded goods sector suggest to Slaughter (2000, p. 148) that the international instruments used by Harrigan and Balaban might be weak. In reviewing the Harrigan-Balaban analysis, Feenstra (2004, p. 132) also points out that international forces still could have brought about the wage changes in the nontraded goods sectors. Specifically, an outflow of capital in response to attractive foreign investment opportunities could have increased the relative wages of skilled labor, thereby raising the prices of skill-intensive nontradable goods and lowering the prices of unskilled-intensive goods.

Conclusion from Studies of Stolper-Samuelson Effects

The different variations on the basic methodologies followed by the various authors, and the different data sets and time periods they analyze make it difficult to draw firm conclusions from their collective work. One conclusion that can be drawn, however, is that the findings from some of the earliest studies that changes in trade policy and in the composition of goods traded internationally do not affect relative factor returns in the manner predicted by the Stolper-Samuelson theorem need to be modified. For example, recent political economy studies, such as Beaulieu and C. Magee (2004) and Scheve and Slaughter (2001), using more detailed data sets than utilized in S. Magee's 1980 study, find that the relative abundance of a factor is more important than the characteristics of the industry in which it is employed in influencing the factor's views on trade policy issues. The findings of more recent product-price investigations, such as those by Leamer (1998), Feenstra and Hanson (1999), and Baldwin and Cain (2000), also modify the conclusions on this subject of such earlier writers as Lawrence and Slaughter (1993) and Berman, Bound, and Griliches (1994). Although the more recent studies find that such forces as unskilled labor-saving technological progress and changes in relative factor supplies generally dominated the influence of trade changes in shaping relative wages during the periods examined, they also find that the pressures from increased import competition and outsourcing in increasing US wage inequality were not insignificant.

As, however, Slaughter (2000, p. 164) concludes from his survey, "research to date still has fundamental limitations regarding the key question of how much international trade has contributed to rising wage inequality." For example, the political economy studies are concerned with what people *think* about the relationship between trade and relative factor prices rather than what the *actual* relationship is. The product-price approach has the drawback of not being able to separate out the effects of product-price changes due to changes in international trade from those due to changes in technology, factor endowments, tastes, and so forth, without making rather arbitrary assumptions. The general equilibrium approach of such authors as Harrigan and Balaban does not attempt to separate the effect of changes in product prices due to changes in international trade on factor prices from other forces affecting product prices.

5.2 Rybczynski Effects

Trade economists have not only been interested in estimating the importance of changes in relative product prices in accounting for the changes in relative factor returns, namely the Stolper-Samuelson effects, but they have also investigated the importance of changes in relative factor supplies in explaining changes in relative outputs, namely the Rybczynski effects. Leamer (1984), Kohli (1990), and Harrigan (1995, 1997) have played leadership roles in estimating these latter effects. In his 1995 paper Harrigan, for example, estimates the effects of endowment differences of capital, skilled labor, unskilled labor, and land among twenty

OECD countries on gross industry output pooled over the fifteen years, 1970 to 1985, for ten individual manufacturing industries.[13] He uses three alternative means for pooling over time, namely generalized least squares with and without country fixed effects, and a time-varying parameter model.

The regression results are mixed. Although the endowments are jointly significant, the overall power of the model in explaining cross-country variations in output is poor. Only the Rybczynski coefficient for capital is statistically significant for all ten industries under all three of the different methods of pooling data over time. The coefficient is positive, thus indicating that capital is manufacturing's friend in the sense that increases in capital tend to increase output in this sector, holding relative prices constant. The coefficients for the other three factors vary in sign and statistical significance depending on the different pooling strategies. In both the fixed-effects and time-varying regressions for all four factors there is, however, at least one statistically significant factor friend—Rybczynski coefficient—and at least one statistically significant factor enemy—Rybczynski coefficient—in 9 of the 10 industries.[14]

One obvious possibility for the poor overall explanatory power of the model used in Harrigan 1995 is that technology growth differs among the sample of countries. Harrigan deals with this issue in his 1997 paper by explicitly introducing relative Hicks-neutral technology differences among countries and industries (as measured by an index of TFP) in addition to relative endowment differences as explanatory variables of an industry's output share of the country's GDP. The empirical framework is basically the general equilibrium model described in section 5.1.1 of this chapter in discussing the contribution of Harrigan and Balaban (1999) in testing for Stolper-Samuelson effects (see equations 5.3 through 5.7 in that section).

Harrigan (1997) utilizes a country panel of data covering ten OECD countries and seven manufacturing industries from 1970 to 1988. Three broad productive factors are considered: capital, labor, and land, with capital being further divided into producer durables per worker and nonresidential construction per worker. Labor is divided into three groups: workers with only a primary education, workers with a secondary education, and workers with at least some higher education. As noted in referring to this paper in the preceding chapter's discussion of modifications to the standard Heckscher-Ohlin model (see section 4.5.3), Harrigan (1997) finds that relative technology levels among countries and industries are an important determinant of countries' patterns of industry specialization. Including this variable also greatly improves the explanation of variations in production across countries and time. In addition the regression results concerning the role of factor supplies are somewhat sharper than in Harrigan (1995). Increases in the endowment of capital represented by producer durables are significantly associated with larger output in five of the seven manufacturing industries. There is also a tendency for larger supplies of medium educated workers to be associated with increases in manufacturing outputs. In contrast, both increases in nonresidential construction and in highly educated workers are negatively related to output in a majority of the industries covered. Harrigan suggests the following explanation for these results: the services sector uses nonresidential construction and college-educated workers relatively intensively so that an expansion of this sector draws these two types of productive factors out of the manufacturing sector.

Hanson and Slaughter (2002) adopt a less theoretically broad approach in investigating Rybczynski-type output effects than Harrigan. These authors explore the importance of changes in the industry mix of output compared to changes in industry factor requirements in accounting for the manner in which US states absorb differential changes in relative factor supplies. Specifically, they analyze the output and factor usage effects across forty traded and non-traded sectors of changes in the supplies of four educational categories of labor in each of fourteen large US states between 1980 and 1990. The educational groups are high school dropouts, high school graduates, those with some college education, and college graduates, while the states included cover the northeast (e.g., Massachusetts and New York); the midwest (e.g., Illinois and Michigan), the south (e.g., Georgia and Texas), and the far west (e.g., California and Washington). Like Harrigan, they find that changes in production techniques play a more important role than changes in relative industry outputs in accounting for the adjustment to changes in relative factor supplies.

The basic equation in their empirical model expresses the equality of factor supply and factor demand in each state and (suppressing state subscripts) can be written as

$$V = FY, \tag{5.23}$$

where V is an $M \times 1$ vector of state primary productive factors, Y is an $N \times 1$ vector of state real value-added output, and F is an $M \times N$ matrix of factor requirements such that each element shows the units of a factor required to produce one unit of value added in a particular industry. They then perform the accounting exercise of taking first differences of equation (5.8) to obtain

$$\Delta V = \bar{F} \Delta Y + \Delta F \bar{Y}, \tag{5.24}$$

where ΔV is the change in a state's factor supplies over time, ΔY is the change in the state's real value added over time, $\bar{F}$ is the average over time of the matrix of the state's factor requirements, ΔF is the change in these requirements over time, and $\bar{Y}$ the mean industry output over time. This decomposition separates a state's change in factor supplies into two parts: change in output mix (holding unit factor requirements constant) and changes in production technique (holding the output mix constant).

Two important relationships that exist in the data on the distribution of high school dropouts, high school graduates, those with some college, and college graduates in the states included in the 1980 and 1990 samples are the relatively wide differences across states in the importance of the four educational groups and the appreciable decline between these years in the employment shares of the two groups with the least education. The labor force in the northeast is skewed toward college graduates. For example, 22.1 percent of workers in Massachusetts were college graduates in 1980 compared to 17.7 percent in the nation as a whole. In contrast, in southern states the proportion of high school dropouts tends to be high compared to the national average. The North Carolina share of high school dropouts, for example, was 34.8 percent in 1980 compared to 25.0 percent for all states combined. The labor force in the midwest tends to be concentrated among high school graduates, with 37.7 percent of Michigan's labor force being in this educational category in 1980 compared to 34.8 percent for the entire country. California is unique in that it ranks high in both college dropouts and college graduates.

Perhaps more impressive than the variation in educational levels across states is the general decline in the shares of less educated relative to more educated workers. In all fourteen of the states included in the sample, the shares of high school dropouts and of high school educated workers decline, while the shares of workers who had either some college or a college degree increase. For the United States as a whole, the two least educated groups made up 59.8 percent of workers in 1980 but only 48.0 percent in 1990. Thus the share of workers with at least some college training rose from 40.2 to 52.0 percent over the decade.

A key finding of the basic decomposition exercise set forth in equation (5.24) is that states absorbed changes in labor supplies in a manner quite different from what would be expected if a shift in the educational composition of the labor force towards a greater share of more educated workers had been the major exogenous shock in the various state economies. In this latter situation one expects the wages of more educated workers to fall relative to less educated workers and the output of sectors intensively using more educated labor to rise in relative terms (and relative output of sectors intensively using less educated labor to decrease) as relative prices decline in the former sectors. In fact the change in output mix among the four educational categories (holding unit factor requirements constant) was negative for the two *least* educated groups of workers in every state. This result, as the authors point out, is consistent with exogenous skill-biased technical change whose demand-increasing effects on workers with greater skills more than offsets the economic effects of the relative increase in the supply of skilled labor and yields the observed increase in the relative wages of more educated workers over the 1980s decade.

Hanson and Slaughter are particularly interested in the role of regional trade and technology flows in absorbing changes in factor supplies. To focus on these forces, they first strip out of total factor-supply changes that part of factor absorption due to nontraded goods. This yields the effective factor-supply changes facing the traded sector. They then distinguish between changes in production techniques due to national shocks from those unique to a particular state. To calculate changes in production techniques that are generalized across states, ΔF_G, Hanson and Slaughter multiply a state's matrix of production techniques in the initial year by the percentage change in production techniques (on a by-industry and by-factor basis) for all other states over the given time period. Changes in production techniques idiosyncratic to a state, ΔF^I, are then set equal to the changes in the state's production techniques minus the calculated generalized changes, ΔF_G:

$$\Delta F^I = \Delta F - \Delta F_G. \tag{5.25}$$

It should be noted that this adjustment procedure permits factor productivity differences across states that are factor neutral across industries. In other words, factor price equalization (FPE) in *productivity-equivalent units* (or what they describe as *productivity-adjusted* FPE) is permitted in the model. It should also be emphasized that equation (5.24) holds as an identity and cannot be used to identify causal relationships among the variables.

Changes in the effective supplies of the four educational groups used by the traded-goods sector vary more widely across states than the changes in the shares of the raw supplies of these four groups across both traded and nontraded sectors. The effective supplies of the two more educated groups increased relative to the two less educated groups in most states. However, in California and a few of the southern states the latter two groups increased more rapidly. They conclude that raw changes in factor supplies may be a poor indicator of changes in traded output. Another key finding is that national changes in production techniques dominate state-specific changes in production techniques as a means of absorbing increased supplies of effective labor. This provides suggestive evidence of *productivity-equivalent* factor price equalization across US states. Plots comparing production techniques between pairs of states for a particular labor category across industries and the two years of data (1980 and 1990) also give the overall impression that the majority of observations are consistent with productivity-adjusted factor price equalization. Furthermore regression analysis of these pairs of observations provides additional support for productivity-adjusted factor price equalization.

It would be interesting to use US state data covering the 1960s and 1970s to investigate the robustness of the Hanson and Slaughter finding that changes in production techniques play a larger role than changes in the output of traded goods in absorbing changes in employment. Unlike the 1980s, the wage gap between more educated and less educated individuals narrowed in this earlier period, with the data being consistent with the hypothesis that a more rapid growth in the supply of more educated workers than less educated workers was the dominant reason for change in relative wages. Perhaps the smaller role that skill-biased technical change apparently played in shaping relative wages in the earlier period may mean that changes in production techniques also played a smaller role in absorbing employment changes in this period. In addition, as the authors also note, a natural extension of their findings on productivity-adjusted factor price equalization would be to compare interstate differences in industry production functions with interstate differences in nominal wages.

5.3 Factor Price Equalization

Both the HOS and HOV models predict that international trade leads to the equalization of the prices of identical productive factors. This relationship follows from such assumptions of these models as identical constant returns-to-scale production functions, identical product mixes, perfect domestic and international competition, and no factor-intensity reversals. The interesting empirical question about this proposition is not whether it holds across and within countries—all agree that direct measurement confirms that it does not[15]—but what the relative importance is of the various reasons why it does not hold. For example, although identical, constant-returns technology may be available to all countries, factor prices may differ among countries because factor endowments are so dissimilar among the countries that they are unable to produce the same set of goods; that is, they produce in separate cones of product diversification. Alternatively, the failure of factor price equalization among countries may be due mainly to cross-country differences in production functions. Moreover, while productions functions may be identical among countries, they may exhibit increasing returns to scale so that factor productivity differs among countries with different levels of production for the same good. Intercountry price differences for similar goods due to trade barriers between countries, the existence of costs for transporting goods across borders, or monopolistic practices by producers in different countries are some of the other possible reasons for unequal factor price among trading regions.

This section reviews selected empirical investigations aimed at determining the relative importance of the possible causes for the lack of factor price equalization. They include not only studies directed at explaining differences in the levels of factor prices among trading regions but at determining the main causes for observed increases in the gaps between factor prices within a particular regions, namely the increasing inequality in the wages of skilled versus unskilled workers in many industrial economies.

As explained in discussing Helpman's non–factor price equalization model (see section 2.5, especially, figure 2.8), if countries' factor endowments differ sufficiently, they may produce different goods at different factor prices even though the same, constant returns-to-scale technology is available to all the countries. Schott (2003a) points out that an important policy implication of such situations is that high-wage workers in capital-abundant countries such as Japan and the United States may be little affected by increases in the output of the goods produced by low-wage workers in China. Consequently, for those interested in the effects of globalization, determining whether countries do in fact produce in separate cones of diversification is a key empirical question.

Schott (2003a) investigates this question utilizing the Rybczynski relationship that if the endowments of all countries lie within a single diversification cone, output per worker in each sector can be estimated as a linear function of the country's capital/labor ratio. If, however, countries are distributed among several diversification cones, output per worker will be linear within each cone but change at each border of a cone. This relationship can be represented as a spline function that is continuous at the cone borders.

Using value-added, capital stock, and employment data for 28 three-digit ISIC manufacturing industries that cover up to 45 countries, Schott estimates via maximum likelihood whether the countries lie within a single diversification cone or multiple cones. Applying a classical likelihood-ratio test to determine goodness of fit, he strongly rejects the null hypothesis of a single cone against the alternative multiple-cone hypotheses of up to five cones.

Schott also recognizes that the typical method of grouping outputs according to similarity of end use does not necessarily combine goods in a manner consistent with a factor proportions framework. Consequently he constructs "Heckscher-Ohlin aggregates" based on the assumption that "the further apart country capital intensities within an ISIC industry, the more likely the countries are to be producing different goods" (Schott 2003a, p. 700). His tests for cones of diversification using these aggregates provide support for the existence of two cones, with the OECD countries in the more capital-intensive cone.

Investigations into the possibility of factor price equalization in the HOV model have also been undertaken based on the extension by Deardorff (1994) of Dixit and Norman's (1980) concept of an integrated world economy (see chapter 4) in which both factors and goods are assumed to be mobile across countries. Equilibrium in such a situation will be characterized by unique levels of output for each good, production techniques to produce each good, prices for the goods, and prices for each factor employed in producing the goods. Assuming there are only two productive factors, capital (K) and labor (L), three goods, 1, 2, and 3 and two countries in the world, 1 and 2, such conditions can be depicted in figure 5.1. The size of the box indicates the combined supplies of capital and labor for the two countries and the slopes and lengths of the solid lines O_1, O_2, and O_3 (measured from O^1 as the origin and arranged in order in decreasing capital intensity) indicate the quantities and cumulated ratios of capital and labor utilized in producing

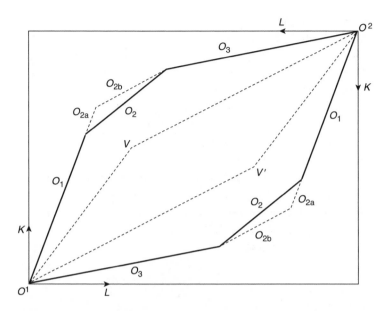

Figure 5.1 Deardorff's factor-intensity and factor-endowment lenses

the three goods in the integrated world economy. Similarly the slopes and lengths (measured from O^2 as the origin and arranged in increasing capital intensity) of the solid lines O_1, O_2 and O_3 depict the same ratios and quantities of capital and labor used in producing the three goods in the integrated world economy. (The relevance of the lines O_{2a} and O_{2b} is discussed later in this subsection.) The area enclosed by these six solid output lines is described by Deardorff (1994) as the *goods' factor-intensity lens* because it has roughly the shape of a lens as the number of goods increases.

Now assume that capital and labor are immobile between the two countries and that each country has particular supplies of capital and labor that add up to the world's totals for these factors. For example, let the point V in figure 5.1 indicate the distribution of capital and labor between the two countries when measured from O^1 as the origin and, similarly, the point V' indicate this capital and labor distribution when measured from O^2 as the origin. The area enclosed by the four dashed lines O^1V, VO^2, O^2V', $V'O^1$ is described by Deardorff (1994) as the *countries' endowment lens* because it also takes the shape as a rough lens as the number of countries in the world increases.

In this 1994 paper Deardorff proves that a necessary condition for factor price equalization in general is that *endowment lens* of countries lie inside their goods' *factor-intensity lens*. He also establishes that this is a sufficient condition for factor price equalization in the case of two countries and an arbitrary number of goods and factors. In such a situation it is possible to distribute the outputs of the three goods produced in the integrated world equilibrium between the two countries in such a manner that the total output of each of the goods and the capital/labor ratios used for each good are the same as in the integrated world equilibrium. Thus the same factor prices and output levels are possible under conditions of free trade between the two countries as exist in the integrated world economy.

A simple example of the many possibilities where this type of distribution of the three goods between the two countries can take place is illustrated in figure 5.2. Assume that country 1 uses its capital and labor endowments indicated by V to produce only goods 1 and 2. This can be shown by drawing a line from V parallel to the O_2 line to its intersection with the O_1 line. Country 2's production of good 1 is indicated by a line from V parallel to the O_1 line to its intersection with the O_2 line. Country 2's production of good 2 is indicated by the remaining length of the O_2

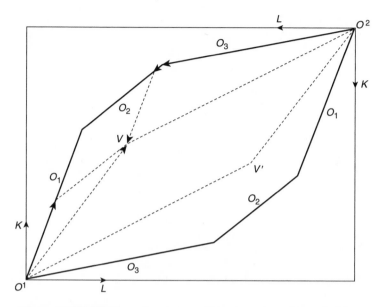

Figure 5.2 Distribution of outputs within factor-intensity and factor-endowment lenses

line, while its production of good 3 is the total length of the good 3 line.

Consider figure 5.3, however, where the *countries' factor-endowment lens* does not lie entirely within the *goods' factor-intensity lens*. In this case, as Deardorff points out, both countries are able to fully employ their supplies of capital and labor using the three available production techniques, but only by producing too much of two of the goods. Country 1, for example, must use more capital and labor in industry 1 than represented by the length and slope of the solid line O_1, or else it will have too much capital per worker to be fully employed in the more labor-intensive industries 2 and 3. Thus factor price equalization is impossible.[16]

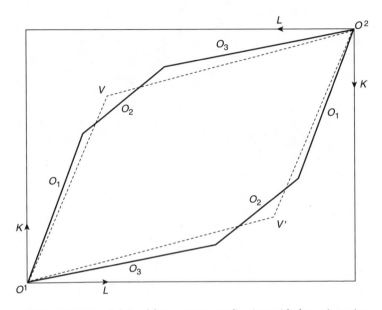

Figure 5.3 Impossibility of factor price equalization with factor-intensity and factor-endowment lenses

Debaere and Demiroglu (2003) utilize the lens condition to investigate empirically whether endowments are too dissimilar around the world for all countries to produce the same sets of goods and thus to lie within the same cone of diversification. In particular, they focus on whether developed and developing countries lie in the same capital–labor cone of diversification. Utilizing data from the United Nations Development Organization (UNIDO) and the Penn World Tables, they construct capital–labor endowment and factor-intensity lens for 28 manufacturing countries and 28 countries. Their finding is that the lens condition is violated; that is, the countries' endowments lens do not lie entirely within the goods' factor-intensity lens. However, when they just construct lens for rich OECD countries, the lens condition is satisfied. This finding is consistent with Schott's (2003a) conclusion that the developed and developing countries lie in separate cones of diversification.

The usefulness of empirical investigations of the lens condition is questioned by Bernard, Robertson, and Schott (2004) on the grounds that lens created by more disaggregate data are larger than lens created by more aggregate data. For example, in figure 5.1, if the capital and labor embodied in good 2 can be divided between two subaggregate goods, $2a$ and $2b$, that use capital/labor ratios different from the ratio used in producing good 2 and that are indicated in figure by the slopes of the lines O_{2a} and O_{2b}, the size of the countries' factor intensity lens increases. Similarly the size of the countries' endowment lens increases by increasing the number of countries if the additional countries are heterogeneous in factor abundance. Thus changing the level of disaggregation of endowments or goods may change whether the lens condition is satisfied.

These authors demonstrate their point empirically using regional data on the employment of skilled and unskilled labor in Mexico's manufacturing sector. Holding the number of factors constant at two but varying the level of disaggregation of manufacturing industries, they find that the lens condition fails to hold when there are 9 two-digit industries but is satisfied with levels of disaggregation of Mexico's manufacturing production into 29 three-digit industries, 54 four-digit industries, and 314 six-digit industries. In view of these results and such theoretical conditions that factor price equalization must be assumed to exist individually within each region, its seems appropriate to regard (as Debaere and Demiroglu 2003) empirical analyses of the lens condition as providing useful information about differences in factor-intensity and endowment conditions among countries or regions rather than as formally testing the possibility of factor price equalization among the countries or regions.

Analyses of factor prices across regions within a single country have also be carried out utilizing a variety of methodologies other than the lens condition. Two recent studies of *relative* factor prices in the United States and the United Kingdom are by Bernard, Redding, and Schott (2005) and by Bernard et al. (2005), respectively. Their analyses are based on a methodology that is robust to unobserved factor-region-industry heterogeneity in the quality or composition of factors.[17] Specifically, let

$$Y_i^r = \delta_i^r F_i(S_i^r, U_i^r, K_i^r) \tag{5.26}$$

be a constant-returns-to-scale valued-added production function for any industry i and any region r, where δ_i^r is a Hicks-neutral productivity shifter that allows technology to vary across regions and industries and S_i^r, U_i^r, and K_i^r are quality-adjusted inputs of skilled workers, unskilled workers, and capital, respectively. (The analysis can be extended to an arbitrary number of industries or factors, where k is any factor.) Individual factors enter production through the function F_1, which varies across industries but is the same across regions within an industry.

Cost minimization implies that the relative demand for observed quantities of skilled and unskilled labor is

$$\frac{\tilde{S}_i^r}{\tilde{U}_i^r} = \frac{\theta_{Ui}^r}{\theta_{Si}^r} \cdot \frac{\partial B_i^r / \partial w_S^r}{\partial B_i^r / \partial w_U^r}, \tag{5.27}$$

where a tilde indicates an observed variable in industry i and region r; θ_{ki}^r is the unobserved quality of any factor k (S or U in this case) in industry i and region r; $B_i^r =$

$\Gamma_i(w_S^r, w_U^r, w_K^r)/\delta_i^r$ is the unit cost function; w_k^r is the price of any quality-adjusted factor in region r; and δ_i^r is the Hicks-neutral region-technology difference.

If quality-adjusted relative wages are the same across regions, (the null hypothesis), observed relative wages vary solely because of unobserved differences in factor quality:

$$\frac{\tilde{w}_S^r}{\tilde{w}_U^r} = \frac{\theta_{Si}^r}{\theta_{Ur}^r} \cdot \frac{\tilde{w}_S^s}{\tilde{w}_U^s}, \tag{5.28}$$

where region s is chosen as the benchmark for measuring factor quality ($\theta_{ki}^s = 1$).

Multiplying observed relative wages and observed relative employment in equations (5.27) and (5.28) results in the terms in unobserved factor quality to cancel. Under the null hypothesis that wages are equalized across regions, relative unit factor input requirements are the same, and thus observed relative wage bills are equalized across regions:

$$\frac{\widetilde{\text{wagebill}}_{Si}^r}{\widetilde{\text{wagebill}}_{Ui}^r} = \frac{\widetilde{\text{wagebill}}_{Si}^s}{\widetilde{\text{wagebill}}_{Ui}^s}. \tag{5.29}$$

If observed regional relative wage bills are not equalized, the relationship can be expressed as

$$\frac{\widetilde{\text{wagebill}}_{Si}^r}{\widetilde{\text{wagebill}}_{Ui}^r} = \eta_i^{rs} \left(\frac{\widetilde{\text{wagebill}}_{Si}^s}{\widetilde{\text{wagebill}}_{Ui}^s} \right), \tag{5.30}$$

where η_i^{rs} is a function of the difference in quality-adjusted relative wages and the difference in unit factor input requirements. Thus a finding that $\eta_{rsj} \neq 1$ is sufficient to reject the null hypothesis that quality-adjusted relative wages are equalized across regions.

The authors' empirically implement their methodology with detailed regional data both for the United States and the United Kingdom. The data reject the null hypothesis that all regions offer the same relative factor prices. In the United States, for example, 64 of the 181 labor markets have relative wage bills in 1992 that differ from the US average at the 5 percent level. A breakdown of the United Kingdom into 10 regional labor markets results in a rejection of relative factor price equalization in 50 percent of the regions in the period 1991 to 1993. However, in both countries they find lower estimated relative wages for skilled workers in skill-abundant areas and a negative relationship between relative wage differences and industry overlap. These results are consistent both with a regional interpretation of the Heckscher-Ohlin model and regional variations in relative living expenses.

The most widely accepted explanation for the lack of factor price equalization is the existence of differences in technologies among countries. The analysis performed by Trefler (1993) demonstrates the appeal of this explanation. In this paper, Trefler allows *all* factors in all countries except the United States to vary in their productivities. The United States is taken as the benchmark country with its productivity for each factor set equal to unity and the productivities of every factor in other countries expressed relative to its productivity in the United States. This procedure permits him to solve for productivity parameters by country and factor that make the HOV equation hold exactly. In other words, the endowments of each country are expressed in efficiency units such that the predicted trade of a factor for a particular country equals the actual trade in this factor for the country.[18]

As stated in chapter 2 (see equation 2.7), the basic HOV relationship can be expressed as $F_k^i = V_k^i - s^i V_k^w$, where F_k^i is the content of any factor k in any country i's net exports ($k = 1, \ldots, M$ and $i = 1, \ldots, T$), V_k^i is the endowment of factor k in country i, and $s^i V_k^w$ is the ratio of i's total consumption to world income (s^i) multiplied by the world endowment of factor k. V_k^w can also be expressed as $\sum_{i=1}^{T} V_k^i$. The HOV equation with Trefler's 1993 modification becomes

$$F_k^i = \Pi_k^i V_k^i - s^i \sum_{i=1}^{T} \Pi_k^i V_k^i, \tag{5.31}$$

where Π_k^i denotes the productivity of factor k in country i relative to its productivity in the United States and $\Pi_k^i V_k^i$ is the country *effective* factor endowment. Trefler measures F_k^i using US total factor endowments and assumes factor price equalization in terms of efficiency factor units. Thus, with data on countries' net exports, consumption, and factor supplies and in setting the productivity of each factor in the United States equal to unity, Trefler's modified linear HOV equations can be solved for the productivities of each factor in each country relative to the United States so that the equations hold exactly.

If, in fact, factor price equalization in terms of effective endowments holds among countries, then the productivity parameters Π_k^i should match the actual factor prices of country i quite closely. Consequently a scatter plot of w_k^i / w_{kUS} (where w_k^i and w_{kUS} are the prices of factor k in any country i and its price in the United States, respectively) against Π_k^i / Π_{kUS} or the ratio of country i's productivity parameter for factor k to the US productivity parameter for k

(assumed to be unity) provides a test of the extent that inter-country differences in the prices of a factor are consistent with the hypothesis that they can be accounted for by differences in the productivity of the factor across countries. In depicting such a diagram for aggregate labor, Trefler (1993, p. 968) points out that the correlation between the two ratios is 0.90.[19] Thus there is strong support for the hypothesis that difference in a factor's price among countries can be accounted for by nonneutral differences in productivity parameters among countries and factors. However, as he also notes, (pp. 969–71), the diagram does indicate that the ratio of the productivity of the poorest countries to the United States systematically underpredicts the ratio of the wages of the poorest countries to wages in the United States.[20] In their analysis of the lens condition for 28 developing and developed countries, Debaere and Demiroglu (2003) also find that the lens condition fails to hold even when all factors are expressed in US productivity equivalents.

5.4   Conclusions

The studies aimed at finding statistical support for the economic relationships set forth in the Stolper-Samuelson, Rybczynski and factor price equalization theorems have generally been less focused and rigorous than those aimed at testing the relationship specified in the Heckscher-Ohlin theorem. The findings of these studies have also been more ambiguous. Thus most of the studies reviewed in this chapter are best regarded as providing useful information about the relationships rather than as attempts to formally test these propositions.

One important conclusion from these studies, however, is that as with empirical investigations of the Heckscher-Ohlin proposition, researchers have generally found it necessary to utilize a modified Heckscher-Ohlin model to find statistically significant support for the relationships expressed in the theorems. In particular, introducing differences of technology over time and among countries has been found to be especially important. For example, various authors of product-price studies find Stolper-Samuelson effects when they allow for the effects of changes in factor productivity. Similarly researchers searching for Rybczynski effects and reasons for the failure of factor price equalization generally find that changes in technology are an important explanatory factor in their analyses.

Some studies have also shown that factor supply differences among countries, especially developed and developed countries, may be so large that factor price equalization is not possible even if technologies between the two groups are identical. Ascertaining the relative importance of differences in technological conditions versus differences in factor endowments in accounting for factor price differences should considerably improve our understanding of the factor price determination process.

The unrealistic nature of the HO model's assumption of perfect factor mobility within countries also seems to be one of the factors accounting for the poor empirical performance of some of the HO propositions analyzed in this chapter. This failure is, for example, the reason given by S. Magee (1980) for his finding of a lack of empirical support for the Stolper-Samuelson theorem when he investigates congressional voting on US trade-liberalizing legislation. Although the more recent studies of such authors as Scheve and Slaughter (2001), Beaulieu (2002), and Beaulieu and C. Magee (2004) do find statistical support for the Stolper-Samuelson proposition in their analyses of political attitudes and behavior with regard to protectionist legislation, their finding that an individual's industry of employment influences political attitudes about protectionism indicates the need to recognize the existence of labor immobility within countries for a better understanding of the forces affecting relative factor prices. Bernard, Redding, and Schott (2005) and Bernard et al. (2005) point to the relative immobility of productive factors within a country as one of the reasons for their findings of significant differences in relative factor price across regions within the United Kingdom and the United States.

6   Conclusions and Related Research Topics

6.1   Successfully Modifying the HO Model

Two notable revolutions in real-side international economics have occurred over the 75 years covered by this review: one dealing with trade theory and the other with the empirical testing of propositions derived from trade theory. On the theoretical side, there was an abandonment of the classical "real cost" approach that combined positive and normative economics in an unsatisfactory manner. It was replaced with a neoclassical framework that utilized the concepts of opportunity cost and reciprocal demand to explain the determination of countries' outputs and levels of trade. The integration of the factor-proportions approach of Heckscher and Ohlin into this framework then permitted trade economists to formulate a general equilibrium theory that tightly tied together product prices and factor prices. The normative side of international economics was separated from the positive side and treated as a part of welfare economics. As Krugman (1994) points out in his comments at the conference celebrating the fiftieth anniversary of the Stolper-Samuelson theorem, these developments stimulated the flourishing of real-side trade theory into a formal, model-oriented field.

The second revolution is the explosion of empirical studies aimed at rigorously testing theoretical trade models and, in particular, tying empirical tests closely to the appropriate theory. Leamer has long been a strong advocate of this point (see Leamer 1984, ch. 2, and Leamer and Levinsohn 1995). His discovery (Leamer 1980) that Leontief (1953) had improperly tested the Heckscher-Ohlin proposition is a classic example of its importance, and the point is now routinely made by empirical trade economists.

Real-side international economists have clearly made enormous progress in better understanding the interrelationships among the forces shaping trading patterns by emphasizing the dual importance of formulating tightly reasoned theoretical models and of rigorously testing the hypotheses derived from these models. However, an unintended consequence of this more formalistic approach—until recent years—seems to have been an overfascination with the elegance of the HOS and HOV models at the cost of minimizing the role of forces other than relative factor endowments in determining trading patterns. The typical real-side graduate text would generally begin with an exposition of Ricardo's one-factor model with fixed labor coefficients that vary between countries, but this is treated largely as a convenient introduction to the variable-proportions HOS model with its assumption of identical technology among countries. After thoroughly discussing in several chapters the basic theorems of this model and the complications that arise with more than two goods and two factors (i.e., the HOV model), the text would then typically devote only a few chapters to other less rigorous theoretical trade models that introduced such features as increasing returns, differentiated products and monopolistic competition, oligopolistic markets, and endogenous changes in technology, factor endowments, and tastes. Given the elegant HOV framework, most trade economists seemed to behave as if there no longer was a strong reason to develop new, rigorous alternative theoretical trade models.

The inconsistency of the empirical results of tests of the Heckscher-Ohlin proposition over a number of decades following Leontief's 1953 test on 1947 US trade data also did little to encourage trade economists to modify the HOV model. As discussed in chapter 3, Leamer (1980) was able to show that Leontief's so-called paradox in 1947 US trade is reversed if the proper adjustment to the US trade balance is made. This adjustment fails, however, to reverse Baldwin's 1971 finding of a paradoxical result for 1962 US trade data nor Brecher and Choudhri's (1982a) finding of another seemingly paradoxical relationship with Leontief's 1947 results. Another example of inconsistent test results is, first, the claim by Stern and Maskus (1981) that the Leontief paradox disappears in 1972 US trade data and, then, Maskus's (1985) demonstration that this conclusion is erroneous. The introduction by BLS (1987) of a definition of factor abundance that differs from the one used by Leamer (1980) as well as by BLS (1986) in their working paper and that gives conflicting results about the existence of the paradox in 1967 US trade data also added to the inconsistency of the empirical findings on the HO proposition.

Trade economists seemed to fully appreciate the necessity of modifying the basic HOV model only after the findings that emerged from testing this model rigorously using carefully collected data on trade, factor input requirements, and factor endowments covering a large number of countries and several productive factors. These findings clearly demonstrated how badly the model preformed. In particular, the findings by BLS (1987) that the signs of the two sides of the HOV equation match only a bit better than 50 percent of the time and by Trefler (1995) that the right-hand side of this equation grossly overpredicts the actual amounts of countries' trade forced trade economists to seek modifications of the HOV model. Interestingly some of those who have made the greatest contributions in modifying the Heckscher-Ohlin model tend to downplay the importance of their modifications. Davis and Weinstein (2001a, p. 1445), for example, remark: "Yet it is startling that such a plausible and simple set of departures from the conventional model allows us to so accurately match the international data."[1] The number of modifications may be small, but by dropping such assumptions as identical technologies across countries and factor price equalization, the extent to which the new models differ from the workhorse HOV model in an analytical sense is very significant.

The main goal of those who have modified the basic HOV model has been to account for the large differences between the volume of countries' factor trade predicted by the HOV model and the actual trade measured by the investigators. In other words, it has been to account for what Trefler has called "the mystery of the missing trade." In undertaking this task, researchers have not relied on well-formulated alternative trade theories but rather on general notions of what might account for the differences between predicted and measured trade. For example, the introduction of neutral technology differences among countries is not motivated by a well-formulated theory that predicts such differences but rather by the fairly obvious existence of a technology gap between richer and poorer countries. The assumption of neutral technology differences among countries is a parsimonious means of dealing with the issue of technology gaps. Thus recent empirical trade economists have backed away somewhat from the earlier dictum that empirical investigations must be tightly tied to trade theory.

The key conclusion emerging from the various modifications to the basic HOV model is that relative factor endowments do matter for understanding patterns of factor trade embodied in goods. Differences in technology among countries generally play a more important role in accounting for differences in countries' trading patterns in productive factors, but once these plus the existence of endowment differences sufficiently large to leave countries in different cones of diversification are taken into consideration, there is significant statistical support for the Heckscher-Ohlin proposition.

As noted in the preceding chapter, efforts to identify Stolper-Samuelson and Rybcyznski effects empirically have been less extensive and generally less rigorous than those aimed at testing the Heckscher-Ohlin proposition. However, investigators have, for example, found strong evidence that in addition to labor-saving technical progress and changes in relative factor supplies, increased import competition has contributed to increased wage inequality in the United States. There has been less success in directly identifying Rybczynski effects.

6.2   Further Broadening of the Analytical Framework

6.2.1   Endogenous Technical Change

Although efforts to narrow the empirical gap between the predicted and measured factor content of trade by modifying the HOV model have been successful, the theoretical foundations for introducing these modifications have not been well explained. For example, given the importance of differences in levels of technology across countries in accounting for the differences between the predicted and measured factor content of trade, trade economists need to broaden their theoretical framework to present causal explanations of why these nonrandom country differences in technology among countries arise and persist. Of course, endogenous growth theory is an enormously complex field, and trade economists can hardly be expected to do much more than adapt the contributions from other fields to their particular models. There are, however, endogenous growth models that focus on some of the same key causal variables as trade economists do, in particular, on relative factor endowments. This presents opportunities for linking differences in relative factor endowments and technological progress.

Grossman and Helpman (1991, ch. 5), for example, formulate a model in which the supply of skilled labor and the rate of technological changes are endogenous. Skilled workers differ from unskilled workers in that they have devoted a certain amount of time to additional schooling. These two productive factors produce differentiated manufactured goods or work in an industrial research lab that produces innovations in the form of new products or quality improvements. Skilled labor is also assumed to be employed relatively more intensively in the industrial research lab than elsewhere in the economy. To illustrate the interrelationships in their model, the authors suppose that there is an increase in the productiveness of time spent in school as the consequence, for example, of an increase in public investment in education capital. Entrants into the labor force who previously were indifferent to becoming unskilled or skilled workers suddenly prefer to become skilled workers, and the supply of skilled labor increases relative to unskilled workers. This lowers the relative wages of skilled workers, thereby promoting an expansion of research activities and a rise in the rate of technological progress. Thus, to quote Grossman and Helpman: "A country that has a greater steady-state supply of the factor most essential for industrial research will allocate more resources to R&D in equilibrium and will experience faster innovation and growth as a consequence" (Grossman and Helpman 1991, p. 140).

In explicitly introducing trade among countries, Grossman and Helpman also present a variety of endogenous growth models that highlight the interrelationships between trading patterns, innovation, and growth. They show, for example, how technological knowledge can be exchanged through trading transactions and results in increased competition among world innovations that leads to a reduction in the duplication of efforts and an increase in the aggregate productivity of R&D activities. But they also explore alternative trading scenarios in which economic integration can reduce the growth rate of a country. Thus, given the significant role that recent empirical work has shown differences in technology levels to play in accounting for differences in trade patterns, it is important that trade economists integrate models of endogenous technical change into their basic factor proportions framework.

6.2.2 Foreign Direct Investment

A key insight of Ohlin that forms the modern basis for analyzing international trade with more than two factors and two goods, namely the HOV model, is that trade in goods can usefully be viewed as trade in the services of productive factors. With this perspective the question naturally arises as to what economic forces determine whether factors of production move across borders embodied in goods and services or whether the factors themselves move across borders.

Investigations of this question with regard to the international flow of goods versus capital have a long and rich history in international economics. Mundell (1957) is a well-known study that utilizes the standard two-country, two-good, two-factor (capital and labor) HOS model to study this question. Beginning with a free-trade equilibrium such as described in chapter 2 where factor prices are equalized, Mundell drops the assumption of capital immobility between the two countries and also assumes that the relatively labor-abundant country imposes a specific import duty on its imports of the capital-intensive good from the capital-abundant country. Since this increases the return to capital in the labor-abundant country, capital will move from the capital-abundant country to the labor-abundant country. As Mundell demonstrates, this continues until the capital/labor endowment ratios are the same in both countries and there no longer is any trade between the countries. Product prices and factor prices return to the same levels that existed in the initial free trade situation with capital immobility. Thus the flow of capital between the two countries serves as a substitute for trade in goods.

Later authors (e.g., Helpman 1984b; Markusen 1984) focus their modeling efforts on foreign direct investment undertaken by multinational firms. Helpman (1984b) analyzes the emergence of vertical multinationals in which a firm's headquarters are located in one country and its production activities in another. There are two sectors and two factors (skilled and unskilled labor) in his model.[2] One sector produces a differentiated product with a constant elasticity-of-substitution production function, while the second sector produces a homogeneous product. A variety of the differentiated good requires a certain amount of skilled labor to cover its fixed headquarters costs and utilizes only unskilled labor in its variable costs. Headquarter services do not necessarily have to be supplied in the same country in which the variable-cost activities are performed. However, production of a unit of the homogeneous good requires both skilled and unskilled labor that cannot be divided between countries. The differentiated product is assumed to be more skilled labor-intensive in its production than the homogeneous good.

First, suppose that the endowments of skilled and unskilled labor for two countries lie in the same cone of factor diversification so that the returns to skilled and unskilled labor are the same in both countries. With the same factor prices and technologies in both countries, there is no incentive for producers of the differentiated good to split their headquarters and variable-cost activities between the two countries. However, now suppose that factor endowments differ sufficiently between the two countries that factor prices would not be equalized if headquarters and variable-cost activities for the differentiated good had to take place in the same country. In these circumstances the relative price of skilled labor will be lower in the capital abundant country. Consequently producers of the differentiated good in the capital-abundant country have an incentive to shift their variable-cost activities for this good to the labor-abundant country, and producers of the differentiated good in the labor-abundant country have an incentive to shift their headquarter activities to the capital-abundant country. The final outcome will be the equalization of factor prices with the capital-abundant country specializing on headquarters services for the differentiated product. Thus the vertical multinationals model associates differences in direct foreign investment among countries with differences in relative factor endowments among the countries.

Horizontal multinationals are firms that have facilities for producing the same product in multiple countries and selling their outputs in local markets. The intuition behind formal horizontal multinational models such as Markusen (1984) and the various extensions elaborated in Markusen (2002) are quite straightforward.[3] The existence of firm-level scale economies are the driving force for direct investment. These arise from such activities as R&D expenditures undertaken in a headquarters location. The improved product or production processes from these expenditures often involve a "public goods" aspect such that the innovation can be used in additional plants without reducing the marginal product of the innovation in existing plants. Thus two-plant firms, for example, have fixed costs that are less than double those of a single-plant firm. These relationships imply that given the existence of transportation costs for shipping the product between countries together with plant-level and firm-level scale economies, horizontal foreign investment will take place between similar countries. However, in contrast to the vertical foreign investment model, the existence of very different relative factor endowments can have the effect of discouraging horizontal multinationals.

6.2.3 Heterogeneous Firms

Heterogeneity among firms within an industry in the sense that they produce different varieties of a differentiated product using the same technology has already been discussed in section 2.4. However, another type of firm heterogeneity that has received considerable attention in recent years is variations in productivity levels among firms within an industry. Interest in this subject has been stimulated in part by the recent willingness of governments to make firm-level data that they collect available to researchers.[4] Trade economists have been particularly interested in determining whether there are significant differences in the economic characteristics of firms engaged in foreign activities such as exporting and foreign direct investment from firms that just serve the domestic market.

The findings from these studies have been somewhat surprising and have stimulated modeling efforts to explain them. Only a relatively small proportion of firms in an industry export, and these tend to be both more productive and larger than those that only serve the domestic market. There are large sunk costs in exporting in addition to those related to undertaking production domestically.[5] Among researchers who developed theoretical models to explain these relationships are Melitz (2003), Bernard et al. (2003), and Helpman, Melitz, and Yeaple (2004). The following discussion summarizes Helpman's (2006) description of Melitz's (2003) model.[6]

Assume a continuum of firms in a differentiated-product sector that each face the same elasticity of demand for varieties sold in the domestic market. The firms differ in terms of their labor productivity (the only factor of production), however. Firms also only discover their productivity level, which is randomly drawn from a given productivity-distribution function, after they have entered the market by incurring a given fixed cost and face given variable production costs per unit of output. For firms with low productivity levels, the profit-maximizing price to charge and the resulting sales will not be sufficient of cover variable production costs plus their fixed costs. They will choose not to produce. But firms lucky enough to have drawn a high productivity level will undertake production and earn a net profit. Moreover the larger a firm's productivity level, the greater will be its sales and size.

Now assume that there is also an export market in which firms can sell their varieties and that the elasticity of demand (though not necessarily the level of demand) is the same in this market as in the domestic market. Trading costs to export markets (e.g., transportation costs and tariffs) are assumed to take the melting iceberg form; that is, more than one unit of every variety must be shipped for one unit to arrive. In addition there are fixed costs in each export market.

The productivity level of some firms that can profitably produce for the domestic market will be high enough so that they can also cover the fixed and variable costs involved in exporting. Thus these firms can increase their overall profits by exporting. Consequently there are three category of firms: (1) those with the lowest levels of productivity that close down because they lose money from domestic sales as well as exporting, (2) those with intermediate levels of productivity that can make a profit by just selling in the domestic market, and (3) those with the highest productivity that sell their varieties both domestically and in export markets. The latter group will also be the largest because of their greater sales.

As Helpman points out, the description of Melitz's model presented thus far is a static version, However, Melitz specifies his model in dynamic terms in which there is a constant probability of the death of every firm, regardless of its productivity level. Steady state equilibrium is characterized by a constant number of firms where the inflow of new firms equals the outflow brought about by the death of firms. This framework permits Melitz to shed meaningful insights on the entrance, exit, and turnover of firms in response to exogenous economic shocks.

Consider, for example, the effects of a proportional reduction of tariffs in all countries. This reduces the costs of exporting and thus both lowers the productivity level at which firms can profitably export and raises the profits of firms already exporting. However, the resulting increase in the demand of labor raises labor costs and forces some of the least productive firms that are only selling in the domestic market to exit the industry.[7] Overall turnover in the sector increases but also so does average productivity.

Helpman, Melitz, and Yeaple (2004) extend the model to analyze horizontal foreign direct investment. In this situation there is a "proximity-concentration" trade-off (see Brainard 1997) between saving on trading costs but incurring increased fixed costs. They show that only the most productive firms will tend to establish overseas production facilities rather than export from domestic production facilities.

A deficiency of the heterogeneous firms models is that a firm's productivity level is just a matter of chance. However, just as researchers discovered that whether a firm exports or just serves the domestic market is not a random event, so too may it be that a firm's productivity level is not just a matter of chance. It may be, for example, that the initially most productive firms are formed and managed by individuals with exceptional managerial and technical skills and knowledge relative to their competitors. Research is needed to better understand both the demand and relative supply forces determining the performance capabilities of different firms.

6.2.4   Other Research Areas

Further theoretical and empirical research on the three topics described above seem particularly important for improving our understanding of the economic influences affecting factor and commodity patterns of international trade, but there are a number of other economic conditions whose relative importance in determining the nature of trade are in need of clarification and further testing. The role of scale economies in shaping trading patterns is a good example. As pointed out in chapter 1, Ohlin sometimes seemed to treat these as being of equal importance in shaping trading patterns as relative factor endowments. Antweller and Trefler (2002) and Davis and Weinstein (2003), whose research on this subject was reviewed in chapter 4, find empirical support for the importance of scale economies in influencing trade and production patterns, but they do not integrate these findings into their general modified HOV models developed in Trefler (1995) and Davis and Weinstein (2001a). Thus we do not have a good understanding of the importance of scale economies compared to other factors influencing production and trading patterns such as relative factor endowments, cross-country differences in technology, and differences in preferences. Research devoted to this goal is very much needed.

A better understanding of the role of demand differences among countries in determining trading patterns and why these differences arise are other subjects deserving of further research. The three best-known, multi-country and multi-factor empirical studies that modify the HO model, namely those by BLS (1987), Trefler (1995), and Davis and Weinstein (2001a), utilize quite different methodologies in analyzing the demand side of trade. As these authors note, all these approaches have their drawbacks, and the authors all encourage further research in this area.

The existence of differentiated products needs to be integrated much more tightly into the modified HO models. As trade theorists such as Krugman (1979, 1980) emphasize, there are usually a number of varieties of a particular manufactured good that are similar but not identical to each other in the many ways described by Edward Chamberlin (1933) in his pioneering book on monopolistic competition. It is interesting that Ohlin (1933, p. 96) pointed out that most manufactured goods were differentiated and that this accounted in part for intra-industry trade.

As pointed out in chapter 4, Schott (2003a,b) finds heterogeneity of output within industries across countries and strong support for the notion that a country's product mix varies with relative factor endowments. Factor-proportions specialization taking place *within* products means that countries may produce in different cones of factor diversification even though they produce goods that are classified as being in the same industry. Additional research in this area seems promising in further developing an alternative to the HOV model that is supported by empirical analysis but is not overly complex theoretically. Integrating the impact of traded intermediates into international models without factor price equalization is still another topic on which both additional theoretical and empirical research is needed, as is the effects of nontraded goods and services in influencing trading patterns.

There have been a number of studies with the objective of determining the restrictiveness of world trade barriers and the benefits from moving toward free trade.[8] However, there have been fewer analyses aimed at assessing the impact of actual trade barriers on the HO theorems. As discussed in section 4.5.2, Staiger et al. (1987) found that their simulation of free trade conditions in the world did not change the ordering of net exports by the United States and Japan to the rest of the world of ten productive factors from the order that existed under actual trading conditions with trade barriers. In view of both much better estimates of existing trade barriers and wider availability of input–output relationships for countries, it would be very interesting to replicate and extend their calculations.

The relative relationship among factor prices is another HO relationship that theoretically can be significantly affected by trade barriers. Section 5.1.2 reviews part of the extensive debate on the effects of changes in trade patterns and changes in relative wages. The most widely accepted view seems to be that changes in technology have contributed most to the widening gap between the wages of skilled and unskilled labor but that changes in trade have also been a contributing factor. There is a need, however, for rigorous studies detailing just what part of the trade changes are attributable to changes in protection and, in turn, what the effect of these changes have been on relative wages.

There are a variety of other topics on which further research can improve and expand our understanding of the determinants of factor and commodity patterns of international trade. But the ones discussed in this and previous chapters seem to be among the most promising. Research on these topics needs to involve both theoretical and empirical analyses. As Leamer and Levinsohn (1995) emphasize in their *Handbook* article, trade theorists have traditionally been little influenced by the work of trade empiricists. The dominance on the theoretical side for many years of the unmodified HOV model, despite growing empirical evidence of its inadequacy as a stand-alone explanation of trading patterns, is a manifestation of this separation of theoretical and empirical analyses in the trade field. Fortunately, much of the recent research reviewed in this monograph indicates that this separation of theory and empirics is changing.

Notes

Chapter 1

1. Ohlin first set forth his trade theory in 1924 in his Swedish doctoral dissertation, *Handelns Teori* (Theory of Trade). This work has been translated by Harry Flam and M. June Flanders and published in their edited book, *Heckscher-Ohlin Trade Theory* (1991). Heckscher's paper, "The Effect of Foreign Trade on the Distribution of Income," was published in Swedish in 1919. An abbreviated English translation appeared in 1950 in *Readings in the Theory of International Trade*, a series of papers selected by a committee of the American Economic Association, while a complete translation of the paper is in Flam and Flanders (1991).

2. In his distinguished survey of trade theories from the time of English mercantilism through the 1930s, Viner (1955) points out that some classical economists briefly mentioned the role of relative factor endowments in influencing trade patterns, but these writers did not investigate the implications of this relationship in the depth that Heckscher and Ohlin did.

3. Unfortunately, in the text of his book, he does not discuss such a situation in any detail.

4. In their excellent introductory essay to their book containing English translations of both Heckscher's 1919 article and Ohlin's 1924 PhD thesis, Flam and Flanders comment that Ohlin "completely ignores the very mechanisms of his own neoclassical, many-factor model that could operate in the direction of preventing specialization and affecting factor price equalization." They conclude: "His motivation here remains a mystery to us." See Flam and Flanders (1991, p. 16) for both quotes.

5. Three notable surveys that cover the testing of Heckscher-Ohlin models are Stern (1975), Deardorff (1984), and Leamer and Levinsohn (1995).

6. The fit between predicted and actual trade also improves.

7. Trefler (1993) demonstrates the importance of country-specific, technologically nonneutral productivity differences among productive factors by performing the interesting exercise of using the data to fit productivity differences that make such a modified HOV model fit exactly and then showing that there is a close correspondence between these estimates and actual factor returns in the countries.

8. I am indebted to one of the readers for the phrasing of this thought.

Chapter 2

1. Viner (1955, p. 520) credits Haberler with being the first economist to set forth the opportunity cost theory as a substitute for the doctrine of comparative real costs.

2. Since adherents to a real cost theory of value maintained that market prices are proportional (at least roughly) to real costs (or the subjective disutilities involved in supplying productive services), they believed that welfare judgments could be made on the basis of market prices, independently of consumer choice. See Caves (1960, ch. 8) for a detailed discussion of the real cost versus opportunity cost approach to the analysis of international trade.

3. Edgeworth (1894) and Marshall (1949) had popularized depicting the production set available to a country with a given technology and factor endowments in terms of a two-commodity, increasing cost production possibilities curve and the country's willingness to trade in terms of reciprocal demand or offer curves. Edgeworth (1894) had also pointed out how the utility received by an individual from two commodities could be depicted in terms of indifference curves. Baldwin (1948) showed how a country's production possibilities curve, reciprocal demand curve, and indifference curve set can be integrated into a single diagram to show these equilibrium values under competitive as well as monopoly conditions.

4. Deardorff (1994) describes this statement of the theorem as the "essential" version. Other versions within the two-good, two-factor HO framework focus on the changes in the relative prices of the two factors brought about by product-price changes due just to changes in trade policy.

5. That the curve is concave to the origin can be illustrated by considering the point H on the diagonal O_1BHO_2 in figure 2.1. The distance O_1BH is roughly 53 percent of the distance between the points O_1 and O_2 so that the output of good 1 at H is roughly 53 percent of the output of good 1 when all the capital and labor is devoted to this good's production at the point O_2 and the output of good 2 is roughly 47 percent of the output of good 2 when the entire supply of capital and labor is used in producing this good at the point O_1. These output levels are represented in figure 2.2 by the point H on the dashed line PHP'. In figure 2.1 the isoquants for goods 1 and 2 passing through H intersect in the manner shown (since H is not on the Pareto efficiency locus) and form a lens through which parts of the Pareto efficiency locus O_1NMO_2 passes. The outputs of both goods 1 and 2 along the optimal output curve passing within this lens are greater than at the point H and can be indicated in figure 2.2 by points on the production possibilities frontier $PNMP'$ to the northeast of the point H.

6. Savosnick (1958) presents a geometric technique for transforming the relationships that exist between two goods along the optimum expansion path in the box diagram to a diagram (e.g., figure 2.2) whose vertical and horizontal axes measure the outputs of the two goods. In figure 2.2 the scales for measuring the outputs of goods 1 and 2 (y_1 and y_2) are chosen such that the distance along the vertical axis in figure 2.2 indicating the output of good 2 when all the country's capital and labor are employed in producing y_2 (OP) is the same as the distance along the horizontal axis in figure 2.2 indicating the output of good 1 when all the country's capital and labor are used to produce y_1 (OP'). Now consider what the outputs of y_1 and y_2 are at the point N in figure 2.1. The northeast extension of the y_1 isoquant at this point crosses the diagonal line O_1O_2 at H. As explained in the preceding note, the output of y_1 at H equals the known output of y_1 at O_2 times the ratio of the distance O_1H to the distance O_1O_2. The y_2 isoquant at N in figure 2.1 passes through the diagonal line O_1O_2 at the point B. Consequently the output of y_2 at B equals the ratio of the distance O_2B to the distance O_1O_2 multiplied by the known output of y_2 at O_1. These outputs are represented in figure 2.2 as the point N. Other outputs along the optimum expansion curve in figure 2.1 can be determined in the same manner, given the intersections of their y_1 and y_2 isoquants with the diagonal O_1O_2.

7. This and the other correspondence referred to below are reproduced at the outset of the conference volume edited by Deardorff and Stern (1994), which celebrated the golden jubilee of the Stolper-Samuelson theorem. See Deardorff (1994) for a detailed discussion of different versions, proofs, and generalizations of the theorem.

8. Although the cause of the price change does not affect the Stolper-Samuelson results, one must, of course, consider the matter of how the tariff revenue is spent if one assumes the price change is due to a change in the level of a tariff.

9. See Deardorff (1994) for a detailed discussion of different versions, proofs, and generalizations of the theorem.

10. As Jones (1965a) notes, Samuelson (1953–54) had earlier shown that the Rybczynski relationship follows from the Stolper-Samuelson relationship, but he did not specifically make this point.

11. If the change in the supply of the factor is not mathematically "small," but instead is a large discrete quantity, the assumption of no factor-intensity reversals in the two production functions (i.e., the relative intensity ordering of the two factors changes over the range of possible of relative factor prices) is also required.

12. Of course, the supply of one factor, capital in this case, does not change at all.

13. If the capital supply is increased, holding the labor supply and relative product prices fixed, there would be a negatively sloped Rybczynski line passing through N that is steeper than the one shown in figure 2.4.

14. As in the discussion of the Stolper-Samuelson and Rybczynski theorems, good 2 is assumed to utilize capital more intensively (and labor less intensively) in production than good 1.

15. These geometric relationships hold for any capital/labor endowment ratio for the foreign country that is less than the capital/labor ratio for the home country and where there is a point on the foreign country's production possibilities frontier with the same slope as the slope of the home country's production possibilities frontier at the latter's autarky point.

16. The actual free trade equilibrium price of good 1 in terms of good 2 and the equilibrium volume of trade are determined by first deriving the home country's offers of good 2 for good 1 at relative prices for good 1 less than this country's autarky price and matching these against the offers of good 1 for good 2 by the foreign country at relative prices for good 1 greater than its autarky level. For a particular relative price of good 1, the home (foreign) country's offer of good 2 for good 1 (of good 1 for good 2) can be found in figure 2.6 by setting a relative price line equal to the slope of the home (foreign) country's production possibilities curve and extending this line in a southeast (northwest) direction until it is tangent to one of the country's social indifference curves. The intersection of the two offer curves

derived in this manner yields the market-clearing equilibrium price and trade levels as well as the equilibrium production and consumption levels.

17. As Samuelson notes, Heckscher was free of this fallacy in his 1919 article. While Heckscher thought that factor price equalization was "generally inconceivable" (see Flam and Flanders 1991, p. 57), he attributed this largely to the absence of the same techniques of production in different countries rather than to some logical impossibility.

18. Samuelson (1953–54) had earlier made the general point about the indeterminacy of production and trade when the number of commodities exceeds the number of factors.

19. Although Travis (1964) derived the basic Vanek equation relating the net exports of a country in a particular factor to its endowment of this factor minus its consumption of the factor (see pp. 102–103), he did not explicitly state its implications for the relationship between the ordering of a country's factor endowments relative to the world's endowments of these factors and the ordering of its trade in these factors relative to the world's endowments of the factors. Apparently, because of this failure to appreciate fully the importance of his generalizations to many goods and many factors, he is seldom mentioned today as an important contributor to modern trade theory.

20. Of course, if endowments, tastes, technology, and so forth, are identical among countries, there is no international trade in goods.

21. See Feenstra (2004, ch. 1) for a more detailed explanation.

22. By drawing a dashed line in figure 2.8 parallel to country 1's unit cost line for optimally producing commodities 1 and 2 (i.e., $w^1 L + r^1 K = 1$) through the quantities of capital and labor used by country 2 to produce good 3, for example, it can be seen that the cost to country 1 of producing commodity 3 at country 1's factor prices with the quantities of capital and labor used by country 2 to do so is greater than one dollar, since the dashed line is above and to the right of the unit-cost line, $w^1 L + r^1 K = 1$.

23. In his 1933 book, Ohlin discusses the limited divisibility of productive factors in his third chapter entitled "Another Condition of Interregional Trade."

24. In discussing qualitative differences among factors, he cites the following example: "A few engineers in one country may have a special knowledge of a particular technical process—or may have patent rights to its exclusive use—and may for that reason, or chiefly for it, be able to produce more cheaply than other countries. In such cases it is no doubt best to

regard the different kinds of technical service rendered as an expression of a qualitative difference between the engineers of such importance that they are to be treated as separate sub-factors." (Ohlin, p. 90)

Chapter 3

1. By "early" empirical tests of the Heckscher-Ollin proposition, I am referring to the period between Leontief's initial test in 1953 and the articles by Leamer (1980) and Brecher and Choudhri (1982a) pointing out that Leontief-type tests are flawed as a general methodology for testing the Heckscher-Ohin proposition in a multi-good, multi-factor framework.

2. Leontief's explanation of the paradox was not generally accepted, since the very large advantage of US labor relative to capital was not supported by direct studies of relative labor efficiency. See Kreinen (1965).

3. As discussed in the next section, this does not necessarily follow if trade is not balanced. However, the Vanek theorem that $F_k^i = V_k^i - (C^i/C^W)V_k^W$, holds in the cases of balanced or unbalanced trade.

4. See, however, the discussion in section 4.5.2 of the much more rigorous test of the relative importance of trade on the factor content of trade by Staiger, Deardorff, and Stern (1987); also see Harrigan (1993). Harrigan found that tariffs and transport costs were more substantial barriers to 1983 imports in OECD countries than were nontariff trade barriers.

5. To establish this point, Leamer used the data on total exports and imports reported by Leontief in his original article and estimates of the total amounts of capital and labor embodied in US production in 1947 that Travis (1964) had made based on Leontief's 1947 capital and labor coefficients for US industries. These data reveal the capital/labor ratio of net exports to be $11,783, the capital/labor consumption ratio to be $6,737, and the capital/labor ratio embodied in production to be $6949. Thus the United States is revealed to be capital abundant because both the capital/labor ratio of net exports is greater than the capital/labor ratio in consumption and the capital/labor ratio in production is greater than the capital/labor ratio in consumption.

6. See footnotes to his table 2.

7. See Leamer (1980, p. 502 n. 2).

8. The calculations by Maskus (1985) indicate that in 1958, when the United States exported both capital and labor embodied in its trade, the ratio of capital embodied in net exports to the labor embodied in net exports was

$8,411 and the ratio of the country's endowment of capital to endowment of labor was $13,278. As Leamer (1980) pointed out, this relationship reveals the country to be labor abundant. Moreover in 1972 when the US imported both capital and labor embodied in its trade, the trade ratio ($22,636) was greater than the endowment ratio ($22,276). Leamer noted that this too reveals the country to be labor abundant. Labor abundance is also revealed by the fact that the ratios of the endowments of capital to labor were less than the ratios of the total consumption of capital embodied in goods to labor embodied in goods in both years, namely $13,278 to $13,382 in 1958 and $22,276 to $22,311.

9. In an earlier paper, Stern and Maskus (1981), Maskus concluded that the Leontief paradox had disappeared for the United States by 1972. However, in his 1985 article, Maskus pointed out that the 1981 paper inappropriately measured output as value of shipments and thus counted intermediate inputs twice. However, Trefler (1995) continued to cite the Stern and Maskus 1981 article to maintain that the Leontief paradox had disappeared in the United States by 1972.

10. BLS pointed out that the HOV equations for capital and labor can be expressed as $F_K^i/K^i = 1 - (s^i K^w/K^i)$ and $F_L^i/L^i = 1 - (s^i L^w/L^i)$, respectively, and further noted that given the assumptions of the HOV model, the ordering of net exports to country-endowment ratios for factors conform to the ordering of the ratios of a country's endowment of factors to the world's endowment of these factors. Consequently, if $F_K^i/K^i < F_L^i/L^i$, then $K^i/K^W < L^i/L^W$ and $K^i/L^i < K^W/L^W$. Since countries consume capital and labor in the same ratio as the world's endowments of these factors under the assumptions of the HOV model, $F_K^i/K^i < F_L^i/L^i$ also implies $K^i/L^i < K^C/L^C$. It is this relationship between the later two ratios (and their equivalent expressions) on which Leamer (1980) focused in reexamining Leontief's conclusions from US trade, production and consumption data for 1947.

11. Leamer and Levinsohn (1995) also used this definition of relative factor abundance in their empirical survey of trade theories.

12. Kohler (1991) also pointed out that a sign or rank-order conflict can arise with different relative-abundance measures of two factors.

13. Casas and Choi (1985) showed that the paradoxical relationship found in Leontief's 1947 data also disappears if the BLS approach is utilized.

14. The procedure followed by BLS can also indicate an ordering of relative factor abundance that differs from that revealed by Leamer's 1980 statement of the basic HOV equations if a capital-abundant country imports

both capital and labor as well as if a labor-abundant country either exports both capital and labor or imports both of the factors. For a capital-abundant country importing both capital and labor (i.e., $F_K^i < 0$, $F_L^i < 0$), the ordering relationship of capital abundance based on the two procedures differs if $K^i/L^i > K^{Ci}/L^{Ci} > F_K^i/F_L^i > K^w/L^w$. In this case the Leamer HOV equations correctly predict that the country is capital abundant, whereas the BLS procedure incorrectly predicts the country is labor abundant. In contrast, if the country is capital scarce (i.e., $K^i/L^i < K^w/L^w$) and imports capital and labor, the ordering relationship of relative capital abundance differs between the BLS procedure and Leamer's HOV equations if $K^w/L^w > F_K^i/F_L^i > K^{Ci}/L^{Ci} > K^i/L^i$. In situations where the country is labor abundant (capital scarce), the domestic country's actual imports of capital and labor are adjusted to take account of how the rest of the world would have spent the purchasing power extended by these other countries to the home country to finance the home country's imports of capital and labor if they had spent it domestically in the manner specified by the HOV model. If the capital-scarce country exports capital and labor, the conflicting relationship arises if $K^w/L^w > F_K^i/F_L^i > K^i/L^i > K^{Ci}/L^{Ci}$. When the capital-scarce country imports both capital and labor, the conflict arises if $K^w/L^w > F_K^i/F_L^i > K^{Ci}/L^{Ci} > K^i/L^i$. In the first case, Leamer's HOV equation incorrectly predicts the country is capital abundant, whereas the BLS adjustment correctly predicts the country is capital scarce. In the second case, the reverse holds.

15. Leamer (1980) also did not utilize an independent measure of factor endowments. He uses estimates by Travis (1964, app. tab. II-A) of the value of capital and number of workers used in producing US gross domestic output in 1947. These are estimated from Leontief's capital and labor coefficients and industry measures of gross domestic output.

16. These ratios were calculated from numbers provided for each country in Bowen's data sets.

17. Adjusted net exports are defined here as a representative per million dollar bundle of total commodity exports minus a representative per million dollar bundle of total commodity imports.

18. Baldwin also found the sign on the capital per worker variable to be significantly negative, a result consistent with the Leontief paradox. However, when Harkness and Kyle (1975) converted Baldwin's net export data to a binary variable (unity if net exports were positive and zero if they were negative) and applied probit analysis, the capital per worker variable turned significantly positive. Branson and Monoyios (1977) applied the same methodology to 1963 net US trade data using the 1963 input–output table and found this variable to be negative but not statistically significant.

19. Feenstra (2004, ch. 2) presents a very clear explanation of why this is possible.

Chapter 4

1. As Hufbauer (1970, pp. 150–51) pointed out, the countries were carefully selected to exclude nations that specialize to a significant extent on resource-intensive manufactures.

2. One notable difference in using US versus EU coefficients, however, is that the ratio for the United States is above unity, but below unity with EU coefficients.

3. The main reason for this difference is that the agricultural sector in Japan ranks as one of the least capital-intensive sectors in that economy in contrast to being among the more capital-intensive industries in the United States and the European Union.

4. In BLS (1987) the authors defined a particular factor of a country as being relatively abundant in supply, if the ratio of its supply to the world supply of the factor is greater than the ratio of the country's *income* level to the level of world income. In contrast, in their working paper and in Leamer (1980), the factor is considered to be relatively abundantly supplied if the first ratio is greater than the ratio of the country's *consumption* level to the level of world income.

5. An Engel curve shows how consumers' expenditures on goods and services relate to their total resources (especially income), holding prices constant.

6. Of course, if the predicted net trade for all factors and countries exactly matches measured trade, countries are exporting their relatively abundant factors and importing their relatively scarce factors.

7. In the published version of his paper he referred to the relationship as "the case of the missing trade."

8. For example, when Trefler plotted the difference between measured and predicted trade against predicted trade, the points essentially are on the diagonal, thus indicating zero trade. The relative unimportance of measured trade compared to predicted trade is also indicated by the very low ratio of the variance in factor trade to the variance in predicted trade. This is only 0.032.

9. The likelihood ratio and Schwarz criterion measures of goodness of fit improve significantly.

10. Gabaix (1999) claimed that the evidence presented by Trefler is not informative about the performance of this model. Because measured trade is essentially zero, he argued that the productivity coefficients are close to being simply GDP per factor, which one expects to be highly correlated with per capita income.

11. In his table 1 (p. 1036) reporting the results from his various tests, Trefler presented his sign test results with each country's sign weighted by the size of the factor content of trade. In the unmodified HOV model, the proportion of correct weighted predictions is 0.71, and introducing Hicks-neutral technology differences raises the proportion of correct signs to 0.78. But, as Debaere (2003, p. 607) pointed out: "The HOV theory does not tell us, however, that the model should perform better for bigger countries than for others."

12. For example, BLS considered their 0.61 ratio for the proportion of sign matches under the unmodified HOV model as providing "little support" for the model.

13. A coefficient of less than unity does imply a bias toward home goods, however.

14. The sum of the parameters across factors that indicate the influence of a country's capital/labor ratio is constrained to be zero under the assumption that capital/labor ratios do not affect aggregate productivity of a country.

15. A potentially significant problem with factor content calculations in a non–factor price equalization model is the inability to identify from the typical input–output table the country by country sources of imported goods used as intermediate inputs in particular industries.

16. Rather surprisingly, however, they found that introducing factor input differences among countries related only to their differences in capital/labor endowment ratios; that is, leaving out the effects of Hicks-neutral differences in efficiency yields a proportion of sign-matches only marginally better than assuming a uniform input–output technology for all countries.

17. Davis and Weinstein also considered a continuum of goods model in which there is approximate factor price equalization but factor input usage in a given sector varies across countries, mainly due to aggregating goods of heterogeneous factor content within industry categories. However, they rejected this is favor of a multi-cone model because the correlation between

input usage and country factor abundance holds about as strongly for non-tradable goods as for tradable goods. See Davis and Weinstein (2001b, pp. 33–34).

18. Since input–output tables generally do not distinguish the sourcing of intermediates beyond domestic and imported from the rest of the world, Reimer limited the regions to two: the United States and a composite rest of the world (ROW). The ROW input matrix is based on data complied from 52 independently constructed, country-specific input output tables based on the Global Trade Analysis Project (see Dimaranan and McDougall 2002). The data cover 57 industries and are measured in 1997 dollars.

19. Reimer does not report the results of sign tests under his methodology.

20. Staiger concluded that his findings point to the potential empirical importance of theories that explore alternative channels through which endowment differences affect the pattern of trade.

21. The authors employed the US factor requirements in estimating the factor content of trade in both countries. They regard these results as being "weakly supportive of the HO model."

22. The EC was created in 1957 and all tariffs and quantitative restrictions among the original members were removed in 1968. However, Hakura argues that since adjustments to such reforms are slow, 1970 represents a period of greater trade restrictions than 1980.

23. The translog function used by Harrigan is described in detail in section 5.1 when discussing the methodology used by Harriagn and Balaban (1999) to test for Stolper-Samuelson effects.

24. The technology matrixes and factor endowments are expressed in efficiency units. In addition national resources are measured net of resources devoted to nontraded production.

25. Despite the fine level of disaggregation used by Schott, it should still be noted that unit-values generally have been found to be poor measures of prices.

26. A good is defined as a four-digit sector in their OECD data set on manufacturing sectors, while an industry is defined as the corresponding three-digit manufacturing sector.

27. One of this manuscript's readers comments that Choi and Krishna should have excluded domestically produced intermediates as well as imported intermediate. (Helpman 1984 excludes all intermediate inputs in

his model.) In private correspondence, Staiger agrees that domestically produced intermediates should also be excluded for consistency with his model. However, one of the article's authors tells me that excluding domestic as well as imported intermediates does not change their empirical conclusions significantly.

28. Choi and Krishna (2004) pointed out (see their appendix A.2) that the basic Helpman relationship can easily be modified to account for Hicksneutral differences in technology among countries. In an earlier draft of their paper, implementing this modification increased the proportion of correct signs only modestly.

Chapter 5

1. Among the pioneers in the development of modern political economy are Anthony Downs (1957), James Buchanan and Gordon Tullock (1962), and Mancur Olson (1965).

2. This approach is based on the formulation of the HO model first set forth by Jones (1965a).

3. In addition to the exposition by Harrigan and Balaban (1999) this section relies on Feenstra's (2004) excellent explanation of the translog function and its various features.

4. The linear homogeneity restrictions $\sum_j a_{ij} = \sum_l b_{kl} = \sum_i c_{ik} = \sum_k c_{ik}$ are imposed on equations (5.5) and (5.6).

5. See Scheve and Slaugher (2001) for a survey of such studies.

6. See Slaughter (2000) for a comprehensive survey of nine studies using the product-price approach to analyzing relative factor price changes. As Slaughter notes, the product-price approach is also related to that of Baldwin and Hilton (1984).

7. Leamer's classification of low-wage and high-wage workers is based on the concept that wage differences across sectors come "entirely from differences in the mixes of skilled and unskilled workers with the lowest wage sector having entirely low-wage workers and the highest wage sector having entirely high-wage workers." (Leamer 1998, pp. 187–88.)

8. This is consistent with the findings of Katz and Murphy (1992) and other labor economists, who utilize other methodologies to reach their conclusions.

9. Import-price data became available in 1982.

10. See Feenstra and Hanson (1999) for a complete description of the database used for the regressions.

11. For example, when the computer share of the capital stock is measured using ex ante prices, outsourcing explains about 25 percent and computers about 20 percent of the rise in the ratio of nonproduction/production wage.

12. A industry is classified as being skill-intensive (unskilled-intensive) if the share of cost accounted for by workers with at least some college education (13 or more years of schooling) is greater (less) than the economywide average.

13. Thus, with 20 countries and 15 years, each regression is estimated with 300 observations. Each observation is divided by the gross domestic product of the particular country for the particular year. Harrigan (1995) also assumes, it should be noted, that the number of goods is the same as the number of factors and, consequently, that factor price equalization prevails across the countries.

14. In the regressions without fixed effects, there is only one statistically significant negative coefficient among the 10 industries.

15. Trefler (1993), for example, calculates the ratio of the prices of labor and capital in some 30 countries to the prices of labor and capital in the United States for the year 1983. Examples of the wage ratios are Sri Lanka 0.04, Columbia 0.22, Greece 0.35, Hong Kong 0.42, France 0.84, Canada 0.84, and Switzerland 1.04. Capital/price ratios for the same set of countries are Sri Lanka 0.13, Columbia 0.50, Greece 0.45, Hong Kong 0.53, France 0.63, Canada 0.75, and Switzerland 0.62.

16. Xiang (2001) establishes that the Deardorff's lens condition is sufficient when there are two factors, while Demiroglu and Yun (1999) show that it is not sufficient when there are more than two factors.

17. The following description of the authors' methodology closely follows their own exposition of this methodology, especially as presented in Bernard et al. (2005).

18. It should be noted that the productivity adjustment in Trefler (1993) is quite different from the one he makes in Trefler (1995), which was discussed in chapter 4. In his 1995 article, productivity differs among countries but not among factors within a particular country.

19. He also calculates productivity parameter and price ratios for capital and finds the correlation coefficient to be 0.68.

20. Trefler points out that the wage data used cover only nonagricultural activities and that agricultural wages tend to be lower than nonagricultural wages. This coupled with the fact that the agricultural sector is proportionately larger in developing countries tends to bias upward the developing country wage data.

Chapter 6

1. The following quote from Trefler (1993, p. 962) makes the same point: "Once international differences in factor prices are properly incorporated, the HOV model performs remarkably well: a simple productivity related modification of the HOV model explains much of the factor content of trade and cross-country variation in factor prices."

2. The following summary of Helpman's model is based on the simplified version presented by Feenstra (2004, pp. 381–86).

3. The following description of the model is based on Markusen (1984) and Markusen and Maskus (2003). Markusen (2002, chs. 7 and 8) also develops a combined version of the vertical and horizontal multinational models.

4. Usually restrictions are placed on the use of these data to prevent the identification of particular firms.

5. See Tybout (2003) for a summary of the various findings of the firm-level studies.

6. Also see Baldwin (2005) for another discussion of the Melitz (2003) model.

7. Melitz and Ottaviano (2005) introduce a different demand system than assumed in Mellitz (2003) with the result that exit from the industry comes about through increased competition in export markets rather than an increase in labor costs. The supply of labor to the differentiated-goods sector is perfectly elastic in their model.

8. Authors of such studies include Brown, Deardorff, and Stern (2005), Hertel and Martin (2000), and Anderson and Neary (2005).

References

Anderson, J. E., and E. van Wincoop. 2003. Gravity with gravitas: A solution to the border puzzlel. *American Economic Review* 63: 170–92.

Anderson, J. E., and J. P. Neary. 2005. *Measuring Trade Restrictiveness.* Cambridge: MIT Press.

Antweiler, W., and D. Trefler. 2002. Increasing returns and all that: A view from trade. *American Economic Review* 92: 93–119.

Aw, B.-Y. 1983. The interpretation of cross-section regression tests of the Heckscher-Ohlin theorem with many goods and factors. *Journal of International Economics* 14: 163–67.

Balassa, B. 1963. An empirical demonstration of classical comparative cost theory. *Review of Economics and Statistics* 45: 231–38.

Balassa, B. 1965. Review of: *The Theory of Trade and Protection* by William P. Travis, *American Economic Review* 55: 253–56.

Baldwin, Richard E., and F. R. Nicoud. 2006. Trade and growth with heterogeneous firms. NBER working paper 12326. Cambridge, MA.

Baldwin, Richard E. 2005. Heterogeneous firms and trade: Testable and untestable properties of the Melitz model. NBER working paper 11471. Cambridge, MA.

Baldwin, Robert E. 1948. Equilibrium in international trade: A diagrammatic analysis. *Quarterly Journal of Economics* 62: 748–62.

Baldwin, Robert E. 1971. Determinants of the commodity structure of U.S. trade. *American Economic Review* 61: 126–46.

Baldwin, Robert E. 1979. Determinants of trade and foreign investment: Further evidence. *Review of Economics and Statistics* 61: 40–48.

Baldwin, Robert E., and R. S. Hilton. 1984. A technique for indicating comparative costs and predicting changes in trade ratios. *Review of Economics and Statistics* 46: 105–10.

Baldwin, Robert E. 1994. Comments on the Stolper-Samuelson theorem. In A. Deardorff and R. Stern, eds., *The Stolper-Samuelson Theorem: A Golden Jubilee*. Ann Arbor: University of Michigan Press.

Baldwin, Robert E., and G. G. Cain. 2000. Shifts in relative U.S. wages: The role of trade, technology, and factor endowments. *Review of Economics and Statistics* 82: 580–95.

Bartelsman, E. J., and W. Gray. 1996. The NBER manufacturing production database. NBER technical working paper 205. Cambridge, MA.

Beaulieu, E. 2002. Factor or industry cleavages in trade policy? An empirical analysis of the Stolper-Samuelson theorem. *Economics and Politics* 14: 99–132.

Beaulieu, E., and C. Magee. 2004. Four simple tests of campaign contributions and trade policy preference. *Economics and Politics* 16: 163–87.

Berman, E., J. Bound, and Z. Griliches. 1994. Changes in the demand for skilled labor within U.S. manufacturing: Evidence from annual survey of manufactures. *Quarterly Journal of Economics* 109: 367–97.

Bernard, A., J. Eaton, J. Bradford Jensen, and Samuel Kortum. 2003. Plants and productivity in international trade. *American Economic Review* 93: 1268–90.

Bernard, A. B., R. Robertson, and P. Schott. 2004. A note on the lens condition. Mimeo. Available at http://mba.tuck.dartmouth.edu/pages/faculty/andrew.bernard

Bernard, A. B., S. Redding, and P. Schott. 2005. Factor price equality and the economics of the U.S. CEPR discussion paper 5126. London.

Bernard, A. B., S. Redding, P. Schott, and H. Simpson. 2005. Relative wage variation and industry location. Revised version of NBER working paper 9052. Available at http://mba.tuck.dartmourth.edu/pages/faculty/andrew.bernard

Bharadwaj, R., and J. Bhagwati. 1967. Human capital and the pattern of foreign trade: The Indian case. *Indian Economic Review* 2: 117–42.

Bhagwati, J. N. 1959. Protection, real wages, and real incomes. *Economic Journal* 69: 733–48.

Bhagwati, J. N. 1972. The Heckscher-Ohlin theorem in the multi-commodity case. *Journal of Political Economy* 80: 1052–55.

Bound, J., and G. Johnson. 1992. Changes in the structure of wages in the 1980s: An evaluation of alternative explanations. *American Economic Review* 82: 371–92.

Bowen, H. P., E. E. Leamer, and L. Sveikauskas. 1986. Multicountry, multifactor tests of the factor abundance theory. NBER working paper 1918. Cambridge, MA.

Bowen, H. P., E. E. Leamer, and L. Sveikauskas. 1987. Multicountry, multifactor tests of the factor abundance theory. *American Economic Review* 77: 791–809.

Bowen, H. P., and L. Sveikauskas. 1992. Judging factor abundance. *Quarterly Journal of Economics* 107: 599–620.

Brainard, S. L. 1997. An empirical assessment of the proximity-concentration trade-off between multinational sales and trade. *American Economic Review* 87: 520–24.

Branson, W. H., and N. Monoyios. 1977. Factor inputs in U.S. trade. *Journal of International Economics* 7: 111–31.

Brecher, R. A., and E. U. Choudhri. 1982a. The Leontief paradox, continued. *Journal of Political Economy* 90: 820–23.

Brecher, R. A., and E. U. Choudhri. 1982b. The factor content of international trade without factor price equalization. *Journal of International Economics* 12: 277–83.

Brecher, R. A., and E. U. Choudhri. 1988. The factor content of consumption in Canada and the U.S.: A two-country test of the Heckscher-Ohlin-Vanek model. In R. Feenstra, ed., *Empirical Methods for International Trade*. Cambridge: MIT Press.

Brown, D., A. Deardorff, and R. Stern. 2005. Computational analysis of multilateral trade liberalization in the Uruguay Round and Doha Development Round. In P. Macrory, A. Appleton, and M. Plummer, eds., *The World Trade Organization: Legal, Economic and Political Analysis*. New York: Kluwer.

Buchanan, J. A., and G. Tulloch. 1962. *The Calculus of Consent*. Ann Arbor: University of Michigan Press.

Casas, F. R., and E. K. Choi. 1985. The Leontief paradox: Continued or resolved? *Journal of Political Economy* 93: 610–15.

Caves, R. E. 1960. *Trade and Economic Structure: Models and Methods.* Cambridge: Harvard University Press.

Chamberlin, E. H. 1933. *The Theory of Monopolistic Competition: A Reorientation of the Theory of Value.* Cambridge: Harvard University Press.

Chipman, J. S. 1969. Factor price equalization and the Stolper-Samuelson theorem. *International Economic Review* 10: 399–406.

Choi, Y.-S., and P. Krishna. 2004. The factor content of bilateral trade: An empirical test. *Journal of Political Economy* 112: 887–914.

Clark, C. 1940. *The Conditions of Economic Progress.* London: Macmillan.

Clark, C. 1951. *The Conditions of Economic Progress, 2nd ed.* London: Macmillan.

Davis, D. E., D. E. Weinstein, S. C. Bradford, and K. Shimpo. 1997. Using international and Japanese regional data to determine when the factor abundance theory of trade works. *American Economic Review* 87: 421–46.

Davis, D. R., and D. E. Weinstein. 2001a. An account of global factor trade. *American Economic Review* 91: 1423–53.

Davis, D. R., and D. E. Weinstein. 2001c. Do factor endowments matter for North–North trade. NBER working paper 8516. Cambridge, MA.

Davis, D. E., and D. E. Weinstein. 2001b. The factor content of trade. NBER working paper 8637. Cambridge, MA.

Davis, D. R., and D. E. Weinstein. 2003. Market access, economic geography and comparative advantage: An empirical assessment. *Journal of International Economics* 59: 1–23.

Deardorff, A. V. 1979. Weak links in the chain of comparative advantage. *Journal of International Economics* 9: 197–209.

Deardorff, A. V. 1982. The general validity of the Heckscher-Ohlin theorem. *American Economic Review* 72: 683–94.

Deardorff, A. V. 1984. Testing trade theories and predicting trade flows. In R. Jones and P. Kenen, eds., *Handbook of International Economics*, vol. 1. Amsterdam: North-Holland, pp. 467–518.

Deardorff, A. V. 1994. Overview of the Stolper-Samuelson theorem. In A. Deardorff and R. Stern, eds., *The Stolper-Samuelson Theorem: A Golden Jubilee.* Ann Arbor: University of Michigan Press.

Deardorff, A. V. 1994. The possibility of factor price equalization, revisited. *Journal of International Economics* 36: 167–75.

Deardorff, A. V., and R. M. Stern, eds. 1994. *The Stolper-Samuelson Theorem: A Golden Jubilee*. Ann Arbor: University of Michigan Press.

Debaere, P. 2003. Relative factor abundance and trade. *Journal of Political Economy* 111: 589–610.

Debaere, P., and U. Demiroglu. 2003. On the similarity of country endowments. *Journal of International Economics* 59: 101–36.

Demiroglu, U., and K. K. Yun. 1999. The lens condition for factor price equalization. *Journal of International Economics* 47: 449–56.

Dimaranan, B. D., and R. E. McDougall, eds. 2002. *Global Trade, Assistance, and Prottection: The GTAP 5 Data Base*. West Lafayette, IN: Purdue University Press.

Dixit, A., and V. Norman. 1980. *Theory of International Trade*. Cambridge: Cambridge University Press.

Dollar, D., E. N. Wolff, and W. J. Baumol. 1988. The factor price equalization model and industry labor productivity: An empirical test across countries. In R. C. Feenstra, ed., *Empirical Methods for International Trade*. Cambridge: MIT Press.

Downs, A. 1957. *An Economic Theory of Democracy*. New York: Harper Row.

Executive Office of the President. 1998. *Economic Report of the President*. Washington: Government Printing Office.

Edgeworth, F. Y. 1894. The theory of international values, I. *Economic Journal* 4: 35–50.

Edgeworth, F. Y. 1894. The theory of international values, II. *Economic Journal* 4: 424–43.

Edgeworth, F. Y. 1894. The theory of international values, III. *Economic Journal* 4: 606–38.

Ellis, H., and L. A. Metzler, eds. 1950. *Readings in the Theory of International Trade*. London: Allen and Unwin.

Ellsworth, P. T. 1938. *International Economics*. New York: Macmillan.

Ethier, W. J. 1974. Some of the theorems of international trade with many goods and factors. *Journal of International Economics* 4: 199–206.

Ethier, W. J. 1982. The general role of factor intensity in the theorems of international trade. *Economic Letters* 10: 337–42.

Ethier, W. J. 1983. *Modern International Economics*. New York: Norton.

Ethier, W. J. 1984. Higher dimensional issues in international trade. In R. Jones and P. Kenen, eds., *Handbook of International Economics*. Amsterdam: North-Holland.

Ethier, W. J. 1982. National and international returns to scale in the modern theory of international trade. *American Economic Review* 72: 389–405.

Executive Office of the President. 1998. *Economic Report of the President.* Washington: Government Printing Office.

Feenstra, R. C., and G. H. Hanson. 1996. Foreign investment, outsourcing, and relative wages. In R. C. Feenstra, G. M. Grossman, and D. A. Irwin, eds., *The Political Economy of Trade Policy: Papers in Honor on Jagdish Bhagwati.* Cambridge: MIT Press.

Feenstra, R. C., and G. H. Hanson. 1999. The impact of outsourcing and high technology capital on wages: Estimates for the U.S., 1979–1990. *Quarterly Journal of Economics* 114: 907–40.

Feenstra, R. C., and G. H. Hanson. 2003. Global production sharing and rising inequality: A survey of trade and wages. In E. K. Choi and J. Harrigan, eds., *Handbook of International Trade.* Oxford: Blackwell.

Feenstra, R. C. 2004. *Advanced International Trade: Theory and Evidence.* Princeton: Princeton University Press.

Flam, H., and M. J. Flanders, eds. 1991. *Heckscher-Ohlin Trade Theory.* Cambridge: MIT Press.

Gabaix, X. 1999. The factor content of trade: A rejection of the Heckscher-Ohlin-Leontief hypothesis. Manuscript. Department of Economics, MIT.

Grossman, G. M., and E. Helpman. 1991. *Innovation and Growth in the Global Economy.* Cambridge: MIT Press.

Grossman, G. M. 1998. Comment. In S. Collins, ed., *Imports, Exports, and the American Worker.* Washington: Brookings Institution Press, pp. 206–11.

Grubel, H. G., and P. J. Lloyd. 1975. *Intra-Industry Trade: The Theory and Measurement of International Trade in Differentiated Products.* London: Macmillan.

Gruber, W. H., and R. Vernon. 1970. The technology factor in a world trade matrix. In R. Vernon, ed., *The Technology Factor in International Trade*. New York: Colombia University Press, pp. 145–231.

Haberler, G. 1936. *The Theory of International Trade*. London: William Hodge.

Hakura, D. 1999. A test of the general validity of the Heckscher-Ohlin theorem for trade in the European Community. International Monetary Fund working paper 99/70. Washington: International Monetary Fund.

Hakura, D. 2001. Why does HOV fail? The role of technological differences within the EC. *Journal of International Economics* 54: 361–82.

Hakura, D. 2002. Erratum to "Why does HOV fail? The role of technological differences within the EC. *Journal of International Economics* 56: 509–11.

Hanson, G., and M. Slaughter. 2002. Labor-market adjustment in open economies: Evidence from U.S. states. *Journal of International Economics* 57: 3–29.

Harkness, J., and J. F. Kyle. 1975. Factors influencing U.S. comparative advantage. *Journal of International Economics* 5: 153–65.

Harrigan, J. 1993. OECD imports and trade barriers in 1983. *Journal of International Economics* 35: 91–112.

Harrigan, J. 1995. Factor endowments and the international location of production: Econometric evidence for the OECD, 1970–1985. *Journal of International Economics* 39: 123–41.

Harrigan, J. 1997. Technology, factor supplies and international specialization: Estimating the neoclassical model. *American Economic Review* 87: 475–94.

Harrigan, J. 2003. Specialization and the volume of trade: Do the data obey the laws? In E. K. Choi and J. Harrigan, eds., *Handbook of International Trade*. Oxford: Blackwell.

Harrigan, J., and R. A. Balaban. 1999. U.S. wages in general equilibrium: The effects of prices, technolgy, and factor supplies, 1963–1991. NBER working paper 6981. Cambridge, MA.

Hausman, J., and W. E. Taylor. 1981. Panel data and unobservable individual effects. *Econometrica* 49: 1377–98.

Heckscher, E. F. 1919. The effect of foreign trade on the distribution of income. *Ekonomisk Tidskrift* 21: 497–512. Reprinted in H. S. Ellis and L. A.

Metzler, eds., *Readings in the Theory of International Trade*. London: Allen and Unwin. Also reprinted in Harry Flam and M. June Flanders, eds., *Heckscher-Ohlin Trade Theory*. Cambridge: MIT Press.

Helpman, E. 1981. International trade in the presence of product differentiation, economies of scale, and monopolistic competition: A Chamberlin-Heckscher-Ohlin approach. *Journal of International Economics* 11: 305–40.

Helpman, E. 1984a. The factor content of foreign trade. *Economic Journal* 94: 84–94.

Helpman, E. 1984b. A simple model of international trade with multinational corporations. *Journal of Political Economy* 92: 451–71.

Helpman, E., and P. R. Krugman. 1985. *Market Structure and Foreign Trade: Increasing Returns, Imperfect Competition, and the International Economy*. Cambridge: MIT Press.

Helpman, E., M. Melitz, and S. Yeaple. 2004. Export versus FDI heterogeneous firms. *American Economic Review* 94: 300–16.

Helpman, E. 2006. Trade, FDI, and the organization of firms. NBER working paper 12091. Cambridge, MA.

Hertel, T., and W. Martin. 2000. Liberalizing agriculture and manufactures in a millennium round: Implications for developing countries. *World Economy* 23(4): 455–69.

Hillberry, R., and D. L. Hummels. 2003. Intra-national home bias: Some explanations. *Review of Economics and Statistics* 85: 1089–92.

Hilton, R. S. 1984. Commodity trade and relative returns to factors of production. *Journal of International Economics* 16: 259–70.

Hufbauer, G. C. 1970. The impact of national characteristics and technology on the commodity composition of trade in manufactured goods. In R. Vernon, ed., *The Technology Factor in International Trade*. New York: Colombia University Press, pp. 145–231.

Irwin, D. A. 1994. The political economy of free trade: Voting in the British general election of 1906. *Journal of Law and Economics* 37: 75–108.

Irwin, D. A. 1996. Industry or class cleavages over trade policy? Evidence from the British general election of 1923. In R. C. Feenstra, G. M. Grossman, and Douglas Irwin, eds., *The Political Economy of Trade Policy: Papers in Honor of Jagdish Bhagwati*. Cambridge: MIT Press.

Jones, R. W. 1956–57. Factor proportions and the Heckscher-Ohlin theorem. *Review of Economic Studies* 24: 1–10.

Jones, R. W. 1965a. The structure of simple general equilibrium models. *Journal of Political Economy* 73: 557–72.

Jones, R. W. 1965b. Duality in international trade: A geometical note. *Canadian Journal of Economics and Political Science* 31: 390–93.

Jones, R. W. 1985. Relative prices and real factor rewards: A reinterpretation. *Economic Letters* 19: 47–49. Also reprinted in A. V. Deardorff and R. M. Stern, eds., *The Stolper-Samuelson Theorem: A Golden Jubilee*. Ann Arbor: University of Michigan Press.

Jones, R. W., and J. Schienkman. 1977. The relevance of the two-sector production model in trade theory. *Journal of Political Economy* 85: 909–35.

Katz, L. F., and K. Murphy. 1992. Changes in relative wages, 1963–1987: Supply and demand factors. *Quarterly Journal of Economics* 107: 36–78.

Keesing, D. B. 1965. Labor skills and international trade: Evaluating many trade flows with a single measuring device. *Review of Economics and Statistics* 47: 287–94.

Keesing, D. B. 1967. The impact of research and development on U.S. trade. *Journal of Political Economy* 75: 38–48.

Keesing, D. B. 1966. Labor skills and comparative advantage. *American Economic Review* 56: 249–55.

Kemp, M. C., and L. Wegge. 1969. On the relation between commodity prices and factor rewards. *International Economic Review* 10: 407–13.

Kenen, P. 1965. Nature, capital and trade. *Journal of Political Economy* 73: 437–60.

Kohler, W. 1991. How robust are sign and rank order tests of the Hecksher-Ohlin-Vanek theorem? *Oxford Economic Papers* 43: 158–71.

Kohli, U. 1990. Price and quantity elasticities in foreign trade. *Economic Letters* 33: 277–81.

Kohli, U. 1991. *Technology, Duality, and Foreign Trade: The GNP Function and the U.S. Demand for Imports and Supply of Exports*. Ann Arbor: University of Michigan Press.

Kravis, I. 1956. Wages and foreign trade. *Review of Economics and Statistics* 38: 14–30.

Kreinin, M. 1965. Comparative labor effectiveness and the Leontief scarce factor paradox. *American Economic Review* 55: 131–40.

Krugman, P. R. 1979. Increasing returns, monopolistic competition, and international trade. *Journal of International Economics* 9: 469–79.

Krugman, P. R. 1980. Scale economies, product differentiation, and the pattern of trade. *American Economic Review* 70: 950–59.

Krugman, P., and R. Lawrence. 1994. Trade, jobs, and wages. *Scientific American* 270: 44–49.

Krugman, P. R. 1994. Stolper-Samuelson and the victory of formal economics. In A. Deardorff and R. Stern, eds., *The Stolper-Samuelson Theorem: A Golden Jubilee*. Ann Arbor: University of Michigan Press.

Lancaster, K. 1980. Intraindustry trade under perfect monopolistic competition. *Journal of International Economics* 10: 151–75.

Lawrence, R. Z., and M. J. Slaughter. 1993. International trade and American wages in the 1980s: Giant sucking sound or small hiccup?" In M. N. Baily and G. Winnston, eds., *Brookings Papers on Economic Activity, Microeconomics* 2: 161–211.

Leamer, E. E. 1980. The Leontief paradox, reconsidered. *Journal of Political Economy* 88: 495–503.

Leamer, E. E. 1984. *Sources of Comparative Advantage: Theory and Evidence*. Cambridge: MIT Press.

Leamer, E. E., and H. P. Bowen. 1981. Cross-section tests of the Heckscher-Ohlin theorem. *American Economic Review* 71: 1037–40.

Leamer, E. E., and J. Levinsohn. 1995. International trade theory: The evidence. In G. Grossman and K. Rogoff, eds., *Handbook of International Economics* 3: 1339–94.

Leamer, E. E. 1998. In Search of Stolper-Samuelson linkages between international trade and wages. In S. Collins, ed., *Imports, Exports, and the American Worker*. Washington: Brookings Institution Press.

Leontief, W. 1933. The use of indifference curves in the analysis of foreign trade. *Quarterly Journal of Economics* 47: 493–503.

Leontief, W. 1953. Domestic production and foreign trade: The American capital position re-examined. *Proceeding of the American Philosophical Society* 97: 332–49.

Leontief, W. 1956. Factor proportions and the structure of American trade. *Review of Economics and Statistics* 38: 386–407.

Leontief, W. 1964. An international comparison of factor costs and factor use: A review article. *American Economic Review* 54: 335–45.

Lerner, A. P. 1932. Diagrammatic representation of cost conditions in international economics. *Economica* 37 (August): 346–56.

Lerner, A. P. 1934. The diagrammatic representation of demand conditions in international trade. *Economica* 36: 319–34.

Magee, S. P. 1980. Three simple tests of the Stolper-Samuelson theorem. In P. Oppenheimer, ed., *Issues in International Economics*. London: Oriel Press, pp. 138–53.

Marshall, A. 1949. *The Pure Theory of Foreign Trade. The Pure Theory of Domestic Values*. London: London School of Economics and Political Science.

Markusen, J. R. 1981. Trade and the gains from trade with imperfect competition. *Journal of International Economics* 11: 531–51.

Markusen, J. R. 1984. Multinationals, multi-plant economics, and the gains from trade. *Journal of International Economics* 16: 205–26.

Markusen, J. R. 2002. *Multinational Firms and the Theory of International Trade*. Cambridge: MIT Press.

Markusen, J. R., and K. E. Maskus. 2003. General equilibrium approaches to the multilateral firm: A review of theory and evidence. In E. K. Choi and J. Harrigan, eds., *Handbook of International Trade*. Oxford: Blackwell.

Maskus, K. E. 1985. A test of the Heckscher-Ohlin-Vanek theorem: The Leontief commonplace. *Journal of International Economics* 19: 201–12.

Melitz, M. J. 2003. The impact of trade on intra-industry reallocation and aggregate industry productivity. *Econmetrica* 71: 1695–1725.

Melitz, M., and G. J. P. Ottaviano. 2005. Market size, trade, and productivity. NBER working paper 11393. Cambridge, MA.

Melvin, J. R. 1968. Production and trade with two factors and three goods. *American Economic Review* 58: 1249–68.

Minhas, B. S. 1963. *An International Comparison of Factor Costs and Factor Use*. Amsterdam: North-Holland.

Mundell, R. A. 1957. International trade and factor mobility. *American Economic Review* 47: 321–35.

Ohlin, B. [1924] 1991. *The Theory of Trade*. Translated and reprinted in *Heckscher-Ohlin Trade Theory*. H. Flam and M. J. Flanders. Translators and editors. Cambridge: MIT Press.

Ohlin, B. 1933. *Interregional and International Trade*. Cambridge: Harvard University Press.

Olson, M. 1965. *The Logic of Collective Action: Public Goods and the Theory of Groups*. Cambridge: Harvard University Press.

Posner, M. V. 1961. International trade and technical change. *Oxford Economic Papers* 13: 323–41.

Reimer, J. J. 2006. Global production sharing and trade in services of factors. *Journal of International Economics* 68: 384–408.

Ricardo, D. 1817. *On the Principles of Political Economy and Taxation*. London: John Murray.

Roskamp, K. W. 1963. Factor proportions and foreign trade: The case of West Germany. *Weltwirtschaftliches Archiv* 91: 319–26.

Roskamp, K. W., and G. McMeekin. 1968. Factor proportions, human capital, and foreign trade: The case of West Germany reconsidered. *Quarterly Journal of Economics* 82: 152–60.

Rybczynski, T. N. 1955. Factor endowment and relative commodity prices. *Economica* 22: 336–41.

Samuelson, P. S. 1938. Welfare economics and international trade. *American Economic Review* 28: 261–66.

Samuelson, P. A. 1948. International trade and equalisation of factor prices. *Economic Journal* 58: 163–84.

Samuelson, P. A. 1949. International factor price equalisation once again. *Economic Journal* 59: 181–97.

Samuelson, P. A. 1953–54. Prices of factors and goods in general equilibrium. *Review of Economic Studies* 21: 1–20.

Samuelson, P. A. 1991. Forward. In H. Flam and M. J. Flanders, eds., *Heckscher-Ohlin Trade Theory*. Cambridge: MIT Press, pp. iv–x.

Savosnik, K. M. 1958. The box diagram and the production possibility curve. *Ekonomisk Tidskrift* 60: 183–97.

Scheve, K. F., and M. J. Slaughter. 2001. What determines individual trade-policy preferences? *Journal of International Economics* 54: 267–92.

Schott, P. K. 2003. One size fits all? Heckscher-Ohlin specialization in global production. *American Economic Review* 93: 686–708.

Schott, P. K. 2004. Across-product versus within product specialization in international trade. *Quarterly Journal of Economics* 119: 647–78.

Slaughter, M. J. 2000. What are the results of product-price studies and what can we learn from their differences? In R. C. Feenstra, ed., *The Impact of International Trade on Wages*. Chicago: University of Chicago Press.

Staiger, R. W. 1986. Measurement of the factor content of foreign trade with traded factor intermediate goods. *Journal of International Economics* 21: 361–68.

Staiger, R. W., A. V. Deardorff, and R. M. Stern. 1987. An evaluation of factor endowments and protection as determinants of Japanese and American foreign trade. *Canadian Journal of Economics* 20: 449–63.

Staiger, R. W. 1988. A specification test of the Heckscher-Ohlin theory. *Journal of International Economics* 25: 129–41.

Stern, R. M., and K. Maskus. 1981. Determinants of the structure of U.S. foreign trade, 1958–76. *Journal of International Economics* 11: 207–24.

Stern, R. M. 1975. Testing trade theories. In P. Kenen, ed., *International Trade and Finance: Frontiers for Research*. Cambridge: Cambridge University Press.

Stolper, W. F., and P. A. Samuelson. 1941. Protection and real wages. *Review of Economic Studies* 9: 58–73.

Tatemoto, M., and S. Ichimura. 1959. Factor proportions and foreign trade: The case of Japan. *Review of Economics and Statistics* 41: 442–46.

Travis, W. P. 1964. *The Theory of Protection*. Cambridge: Harvard University Press.

Trefler, D. 1993. International factor price differences: Leontief was right! *Journal of Political Economy* 101: 961–87.

Trefler, D. 1995. The case of missing trade and other HOV mysteries. *American Economic Review* 85: 1029–46.

Tybout, J. 2003. Plant- and firm-level evidence in "new trade theories." In E. K. Choi and J. Harrigan, eds., *Handbook of International Trade*. Oxford: Blackwell.

Vanek, J. 1963. *The Natural Resource Content of U.S. Foreign Trade, 1870–1955*. Cambridge: MIT Press.

Vanek, J. 1968. The factor proportions theory: The N-factor case. *Kyklos* 2: 749–54.

Vernon, R. 1966. International investment and international trade in the product cycle. *Quarterly Journal of Economics* 80: 190–207.

Viner, J. 1955. *Studies in the Theory of International Trade*. London: Allen and Unwin.

Xiang, C. 2001. The sufficiency of the "lens condition" for factor price equalization in the case of two factors. *Journal of International Economics* 53: 463–74.

Yahr, M. 1968. Human capital and factor substitution in the CES production function. In P. Kenen and R. Lawrence, eds., *The Open Economy: Essays in International Trade and Finance*. New York: Columbia University Press.

Index